Illinois Central College

Learning Resource Center

STUDIES IN MODERN EUROPEAN
LITERATURE AND THOUGHT

General Editors:
ERICH HELLER
Professor of German
Northwestern University

and

ANTHONY THORLBY
Reader in Comparative Literature
in the University of Sussex

DOSTOIEVSKY

ALSO PUBLISHED IN THIS SERIES:

DOSTOIEVSKY

BY

A. STEINBERG

NEW YORK
HILLARY HOUSE PUBLISHERS
(A Division of Humanities Press Inc.)
1968

First published in 1966 in the U.S.A. by
HILLARY HOUSE PUBLISHERS
(A Division of Humanities Press Inc.)
New York
Reprinted 1968

Library of Congress Catalog Card No. 66–15542
Printed in Great Britain by
Fletcher & Son Ltd, Norwich
Set in Monotype Garamond

CONTENTS

I

The Martyr

Truth dawns in adversity.

> Dostoievsky, Letter from Siberia,
> 20 February 1854

Dostoievsky was certainly no saint, but in the entire history of European thought and literature of the last century there is none who more deserves to be included in the host of tormented souls with a halo of martyrdom about them.

Even at a most cursory acquaintance with Dostoievsky's biography, one is struck by the dark chasm which gapes tragically through the very middle of his sixty years of life and splits it into almost equal halves. The first breaks off abruptly in 1849, when, at the age of 28, the young author, having already acquired fame, is condemned to death, a verdict later changed to four years penal servitude and subsequent banishment to Siberia. The second half begins in 1854 and extends over the remaining 27 years of Dostoievsky's life which witness a gradual re-union with his severed past and moulds the Dostoievsky the world knows.

In such a biographical frame, the martyrdom of Dostoievsky emerges, however, only as an isolated chronologically defined episode. This impression is deceptive. The martyrdom of Dostoievsky did not begin when he was brought to trial for activities

7

against the state, nor did it conclude at his reconciliation with the government of the new liberal emperor, Alexander II, successor to the cruel Nicholas I. A careful study of the material relating to the origin, the outward circumstances and, in particular, to the inner development of the extraordinarily distinctive personality of Fyodor Mikhailovich Dostoievsky, unavoidably leads to the conclusion that he was fated, as it were, during his life to suffer grief and anxiety in gaol or in freedom. It is equally certain that, were his destiny different, he would not have left to us that unique heritage we owe him as artist and thinker.

The time and place of Dostoievsky's appearance could not have been better fitted to his predestined role of raising the art and thought of the 19th century to the summit of heroic martyrdom. Had the Russia of Nicholas I not been a historical fact, it would have to be invented to bring together the necessary conditions for the development of Dostoievsky's many-sided creative genius. Where else could have been kindled the inextinguishable blaze of his consuming compassion, if not in the country of legalized bestiality, a country which in the words of Dostoievsky's contemporary, the poet Tyutchev, the King of Heaven himself 'has walked all over in the guise of a slave'? In what other epoch could the life-giving imagination of Dostoievsky, the artist, be as unconditionally subordinated to the tormenting processes of thought than in the period of Russian history when Russian literature, personified by Pushkin, had recognized as its basic task 'the glorification of freedom', and had gone all out to lay down new principles for the people's existence?

The year and place of Dostoievsky's birth, Moscow 1821, and that of his death, St. Petersburg 1881, mark the chronological and geographical poles which encompass the whole sphere of his individual life within the significant epoch of Russian history – from the eve of the Decembrist revolt to the assassination of Alexander II. This was the time when the underground rumble, still subdued but audible to the finer ear, time after time generated violent explosions. The two capitals of Russia – St. Petersburg with its 'window to Europe', and Moscow, in the depths of introspection, began openly to compete for the heart and mind of the nation. There is no major event in that period of Russian history and no current of thought then emerging which did not re-echo in the soul of Dostoievsky, forcing him over and over again to re-examine and re-consider the values he cherished. If the whole of Russia was spread at the foot of an awakening volcano, then the path of Dostoievsky's life ran close to its very crater. Constantly in a state of anxiety, tormented by everlasting fears, he consciously rejected all temptations of a quiet life with others and like others, and very early on withdrew into himself.

Dostoievsky's biographers often try to find the key to his 'complex character' on the plane of accepted psychological or psycho-pathological theories. In their attempts to penetrate to the essence of his personality they use the evidence of his contemporaries or his own testimony, but nearly always

9

leave out of account the most important source – the unique confession of his impassioned and over-sensitive heart, his *Complete Works*. Whatever else the author taught in them about man, all his writings, whether he willed it or not, quite apart from direct references to his own experience, are all an unending tale about himself, about the relentless agonizing craving to know himself, to grasp his true mission and the sense of his vocation. This will be discussed in greater detail in the following chapters on Dostoievsky 'The Artist' and Dostoievsky 'The Thinker'. But it seems that it is impossible to get a closer view of Dostoievsky, the man, without anticipating, at least in part, the results of the study of his work.

The unquenchable thirst for self-knowledge, or rather self-conquest, distinguishes also Friedrich Nietzsche, the German contemporary of Dostoievsky, and in a certain sense his fellow sufferer. But in distinction from Dostoievsky, the doleful German recluse thought that this was an aim within his reach, while Dostoievsky, when hardly eighteen years old, already realized that he might remain an insoluble enigma unto himself. This is what he writes to his elder brother and friend, Mikhail, on 16 August 1839, shortly after the death of their father: 'My soul is closed to the violent outbursts of the past. It is as calm as the heart of a man guarding a profound mystery. . . .' And further: 'Man is a mystery. It has to be divined, and if you will spend a lifetime in doing so, then don't say that it was a waste of time; I am studying this mystery, since I want to be a man.' On the very threshold of his adult life, Dostoievsky sensed that which at its end found expression in his Pushkin speech: he had, as it were, a presentiment that like Pushkin he was destined to carry his 'profound mystery' with him to the grave.

In Dostoievsky's wanderings through the labyrinth of his soul, Pushkin ever remained his 'Virgil'. His eyes ever turning back to Pushkin's shadow, Dostoievsky strove to perceive him as a harmonious whole, as an 'organic entity'. With such an ideal embodiment of a human personality in his mind's eye, Dostoievsky saw himself as the direct opposite of the fulfilled beautiful image of man. He imagined he was a formless mass from which he had to mould himself. The task of self-knowledge, the discovery of his own essence, coincided for Dostoievsky with that of self-creation and self-incarnation. And though such a task can never be finally achieved by anyone, it is nevertheless permissible to inquire in what measure Dostoievsky succeeded in solving it, to what degree he was able to master his own original chaos. Posterity might find it easier to answer this question than did he or his contemporaries, including Tolstoy who at times regarded Dostoievsky as his moral 'support' and at others inclined to the opinion that Dostoievsky's 'mind and heart had been wasted for naught'. We know more about Dostoievsky than he did himself, if only for the reason that we possess in his creations, canonized in the history of world literature, the unintended results, often underrated by himself, of his strivings for self-knowledge and self-incarnation.

The history of 19th-century literature abounds

with biographies of creative men who at an early age became a problem to themselves. But, usually, as soon as they assumed to have found their place within their surroundings, the problem became irrelevant to them. It might seem that Dostoievsky, too, having very early discovered his vocation as a writer and having almost at once met with recognition, would without hesitation have identified himself with his work. But this did not happen. The plain fact that he was a Russian writer, first and foremost, never became a self-evident truth in his eyes. When he was nearly fifty, and after he had already created *Crime and Punishment*, he still doubted not only the significance of his works, but even his claim to a place in Russian literature. (Cf. letter of 14 July 1870 to his niece, S. A. Ivanova.) In other words, 'the mystery' of his youth was not yet unravelled.

It is true that at about the same age Tolstoy also became doubtful whether he had chosen the right way – as indeed had Gogol before him – and finished by indiscriminately condemning all his works of art. But in the case of Tolstoy (as in that of Gogol) this occurred only after a profound inner upheaval, in fact after his famous 'conversion' which prompted him sharply to change the main course of his life. Dostoievsky, however, never experienced an inner revolution. Throughout his spiritual development no crack is discernible, not to speak of a break. His life is spent in constant turmoil and trepidation, in passionate combat with himself; he is tossed from turbulence to turbulence, from one vortex to the next, but always, as it were, within the same appointed channel. A comparison of Dostoievsky with Tolstoy, his near neighbour in space and time and even in the sphere of the spirit, whom however he never met face to face, would best illumine the distinctive individual fate of each. Tolstoy was destined in his own lifetime to witness the realization of all his personal strivings, while Dostoievsky, already on the verge of death, was still faced with agonizing doubts about the meaning of his existence and the goals attained. Tolstoy, the 'realist', started with autobiography, with an accurate account of his 'Childhood'. The annals of Dostoievsky's life are mottled with question marks which he himself put all over the margins and which he never deciphered. This fully accords with the romantic discovery of his youth that man's individuality is a mystery unto himself.

Unlike the early period of Tolstoy's life, the childhood, adolescence, and youth of Dostoievsky appear shrouded in mist. Condemned to lifelong martyrdom, was he ever happy, at least in the first years in his parents' house? Biographers have a negative answer to give us. In the close overcrowded apartment attached to Moscow's hospital for the poor, where his father worked as a doctor, there reigned a severe régime. The gentle and naïvely religious mother of little Fedya tried to soften the stern temper of her husband. But he, the son of a clergyman and a member of the smaller gentry, was irritated against his wife's wealthier relatives of the merchant class. He not only felt poor, but constantly saw himself as the poor relation and sometimes wreaked his anger on the serfs of his small estate. In analysing the character of Dostoievsky, his 'duality' is often emphasized. His noble high mindedness and exceptional kindness ill accorded with his meanness, mercenary pettiness and, at times, even cruelty. Efforts are made to explain these contradictions by the contrasting characters of his parents. This discord is used also to account for the unbalanced emotional state of Dostoievsky which became apparent in his early childhood and slowly developed into chronic illness. If it is true that the curse suspended over man in general can be traced to 'poverty' on the social plane and to 'illness' in the physical sense, then the double curse which pursued Dostoievsky almost all his life overtook him, it seems, already in his adolescence, even before he parted from his parental home and Moscow. A striking confirmation of this assumption follows, it may seem, from the organic aversion Dostoievsky felt for his native city. It is as well to give this a closer look, the more so as the literature on Dostoievsky completely ignores it.

'Moscow . . .' exclaims Pushkin in *Eugene Onegin*, 'how deeply does the very sound stir the Russian heart.' But in the undoubtedly 'Russian heart' of the Muscovite, Dostoievsky, there is no sympathetic response to this name. From the time, when at the age of sixteen he was taken by his father from the Moscow boarding school to be placed in the Engineering College in St. Petersburg, Dostoievsky never again returned to reside in the 'ancient metropolis of old Muscovy'. He quite evidently avoided it. Whenever he went there, he tried to leave again as quickly as possible. Although yearning to return to

Russia after nearly four years' absence abroad, he speaks in his letter to his favourite Moscow niece of the possibility of settling in her neighbourhood, but, it appears, merely for the reason that even Moscow was preferable to being abroad. (Letter to S. A. Ivanova of 26 December 1869.) Indeed, in all his writings he consistently excluded, as a place of action, the city in which he spent his childhood and adolescence. He did not want to be there even in his imagination. There is a most significant omission at the beginning of the second part of *The Idiot*: Prince Myshkin has left St. Petersburg for fully six months. 'But about the prince's adventures in Moscow and during his absence from St. Petersburg generally' – emphasizes the narrator – 'we can give very little information.' In many other works Moscow is consigned to the farthest corner of the horizon and the reader never has the opportunity of finding himself there. It is quite clearly out of bounds. This is all the more remarkable, since in his outlook Dostoievsky was to a considerable extent the follower of Moscow slavophiles and a convinced opponent of the St. Petersburg 'westernizers', as well as of the 'St. Petersburg period' of Russian history as a whole. And yet, thanks to Dostoievsky, St. Petersburg became as familiar to the European understanding, as Moscow, thanks to Tolstoy. Not even the climate of Moscow, incomparably more favourable to the poor lungs of Dostoievsky than the mugginess of St. Petersburg, ('a hellish one' in his own words), could soften his heart. This peculiar preference is difficult to explain, other than by a conscious or unconscious desire to forget a considerable period of his own early development.

However, his childhood years, the ailments and first impressions of the surrounding misery, could hardly account for it. Those years, when his mother used to take him to church and taught him to read from the book *One hundred and four holy stories from the Old and New Testament* (mentioned in *The Brothers Karamazov*, Book VI, Chap. IIb.), those years when his brothers and sisters crowded round him in tender love, remained a 'precious memory' for ever. 'For man has no more precious memory than that of his early childhood spent in his parental home, and this is always true, even if there is only the least love and cohesion in the family' – thus speaks Dostoievsky through the mouth of the Elder Zosima. In that period of 'early childhood' Moscow was the bright festive background to Dostoievsky's grey parental house. 'I come from a family Russian and pious' – he reminisces when over fifty – 'every visit to the Kremlin and the cathedrals of Moscow were always festive occasions for me.' And he continues with emphasis: 'As far back as my memory reaches, I can remember my parents' love for me.' (See 'One of the contemporary falsehoods' in *A Writer's Diary* of 1873, No. 50). In face of this and similar evidence (e.g. in letters to his brothers Mikhail and Andrey), it is impossible to agree that the key to the exceptional complexity of his spiritual structure is to be found in some basic family conflict and not in his own unique nature. Perhaps a more satisfactory explanation might be discovered within this structure

16

itself, in the spontaneous reaction of young Dostoievsky's unique nature to certain aspects of his inner growth. Indeed, was there something extraordinary that happened to him in Moscow?

It seems this can best be answered in the spirit of Dostoievsky himself. Moscow was witness to the end of his 'golden age'; in Moscow he was banished from his childhood's paradise; there occurred 'the fall' which he described so precisely about half a century later in 'The Dream of a Ridiculous Man': 'The cause of the fall was I . . . I infected the entire happy earth, sinless until my emergence. . . . People learned to lie and to love falsehood and discovered the beauty of the lie. Soon voluptuousness was born, voluptuousness brought forth jealousy, jealousy begat cruelty. Then began the fight for separation, for isolation, for personality.' (*A Writer's Diary.* 1877, IV, Chap. 2, V.). Looking back to his own sinless distant past, Dostoievsky discloses how the world had changed for him, when his 'I' was born in his consciousness and the ceaseless agonizing fight began for his own identity, for self-knowledge and self-incarnation.

In the critical transition from childhood to adolescence, Dostoievsky would hardly have been able at once to disentangle the complexity of what he perceived to be his 'fall'. There is, however, no doubt that this transition became an event which determined his further development. Literary criticism gives much prominence to the place occupied by children in Dostoievsky's writing. Their innocence, their 'angelic image' and, especially, their suffering are

B   17

often ascribed to a certain 'perversity' in the author. Rarely does it occur to anybody that in speaking about children, other people's or his own, and in creating children's images, Dostoievsky invariably returned to his own Lost Paradise. Finding himself outside its gates, he began to discern good and evil within himself. He began to blame himself for what had happened to him and, not yet possessing the power to describe his condition, began to conceal his thoughts, to stand aloof and, while still an adolescent, he withdrew into himself. Involuntarily he 'learned to lie' and very soon 'discovered the beauty of the lie'.

In order fully to evaluate the autobiographical significance of 'The Dream of a Ridiculous Man', it should be remembered that Dostoievsky thought himself to be 'ridiculous' at the very beginning of his creative period, when he wrote the *Poor People* and *White Nights*. And as to the 'beauty of the lie', Dostoievsky became aware of it in the earliest years of his adolescence, before even 'voluptuousness was born' in him. While his mother was introducing the children to the Holy Writ, his father read aloud to them Karamzin's *Russian History* and novels by various Russian and foreign authors. The fantastic novels by Anne Radcliffe, of course in Russian translation, made a particular impression on the immature imagination of the children (e.g. see letter of 31 July 1861 to the poet Polonsky). Side by side with the real world there arose in Fedya's lively imagination the world of 'beautiful' inventions and bewitching 'lies', and these worlds collided.

The deeper young Fedya delved into himself, the more acutely he began to be aware of his own 'sinfulness', and the more clearly he perceived the evil which reigned in the world outside. How very far was Orthodox Moscow from the Testament of Christ! How difficult it was to reconcile it to the cruel treatment of the serfs even on their own small estate! And this is when it first occurs to the youthful Fedya that his only salvation lay in escape – escape from the world of reality to the world of fantasy, the world of literature. To cope with his evil inclinations and the torture of his conscience at the sight of helpless victims subjected to the surrounding cruelty, the young Dostoievsky sets a halo on the ideal of beauty. Not the illusory and deceptive beauty, but that which could verily become a 'great force' and 'save the world'. This is 'The Idiot's', Prince Myshkin's, credo which first germinated in Dostoievsky when he revolted spiritually against the morally hideous life around him. Then, at the beginning of 1837, Pushkin, the living incarnation of ideal beauty in Dostoievsky's eyes, was killed in a duel. At about the same time ebbed away the life of his mother who had brought the image of Christ and Christian martyrs near to him. This coincidence acquired a symbolical meaning for the adolescent. Artistic truth, Pushkin's poetry, fused in his soul with the divinely revealed religion of suffering. Only two or three years later he began to put Shakespeare side by side with Moses, and Homer with Christ: '. . . Homer (a mythical man who, perhaps like Christ, was made flesh by God and sent to us),' writes Dostoievsky, 'has a parallel only in Christ. . . . Indeed, it was Homer who gave the entire ancient world its organisation of spiritual and earthly life in exactly the same sense as that given by Christ to the new world' (letters to Mikhail of 16 August 1839 and 1 January 1840). If it is correct to assume that Dostoievsky believed in the saving 'organizational' power of literature even before he departed from Moscow, then it would be quite natural that already then he began to see in the world of imagination not only a refuge from his inner discord, but a sphere in which to apply his talents. He and his brother Mikhail 'were dreaming only about poetry and poets', recalls Dostoievsky some forty years later; his brother was writing verses and he was 'all the time compiling in his mind a novel about Venetian life'. (*A Writer's Diary*, 1876, January, Chap. 3, 1.) It may be appropriate to mention here that at the very end of his literary activity the author of *The Brothers Karamazov* was contemplating 'writing a book on Christ'. Was the 'novel about Venetian life' the first conception of a book in which the perfection of good would be contrasted with the vile ugliness of evil against the shining background of fabulous beauty?

Be this as it may, between the fulfilment of his last dream and the first awareness of his vocation, there stood Dostoievsky himself with his creative potential and the looming menace of the world's evil. The same chapter of his *Diary* in which he recalls his first literary dream, contains an artistically beautiful, yet meticulously precise, description or even definition of the legalized bestiality which characterized the people's life in Russia under Nicholas I. In May 1837, when Dostoievsky's father was taking his two elder sons to St. Petersburg to place them there in the Engineering College, Dostoievsky saw the following picture from the window of a wayside inn. From the post-coach station there rushed out an official courier, 'a very hefty thickset fellow, purple of face, who sat down in the small carriage, then half rose and silently, without any words whatever, lifted his enormous right fist and from above let it fall with a mighty blow onto the back of the coachman's neck. The man collapsed forward, lifted the whip and with all his might lashed out at the middle horse. The horses strained forward, but this in no way reduced the courier's fury. Here was a method, not irritation, but something preconceived and tested in long experience. The fearful fist flew up once more and once more hit into the neck. Then again, and again, and this went on until the troika was lost to view. Obviously, the coachman, hardly able to hold up under the blows and as though demented, incessantly and every second whipped the horses and, finally, had whipped them up so much that they flew like mad. . . .' The coachman, remarks Dostoievsky, on his return home will surely vent his anger on his wife and beat her up to revenge his pain and humiliation. 'This revolting picture' – concludes Dostoievsky – 'remained in my memory for life . . . this picture was like an emblem, like something which clearly demonstrated the connection between cause and effect. Here, every blow that hit the animals sprang forth as though by itself from every blow that fell on the man.'

In this 'emblem' of Dostoievsky we can see the entire chain-reaction which brought into motion the state machinery of the reactionary emperor. The strongest links in that chain were the fist and the knout. It began with the brutal will of the autocract whipping up the tsar's servant, and its final victims were the dumb animals and the almost equally dumb Russian woman. This fearful chain of automatic violence had to be smashed at all costs – how could the young Dostoievsky not feel it? And it was becoming evident that by the 'novel about Venetian life' matters could not be mended. Before ever he stepped into the capital of the tsars, he discovered the citizen within himself and his literary dreams became more sombre.

In the year which saw the violent end of the greatest Russian poet, there could have been no doubt that to dedicate oneself to independent thought and its free expression was tantamount to self-sacrifice. Lermontov, author of the poem 'On the Death of Pushkin', suffered the same fate as that of his hero. Already, earlier, the poet Ryleyev was one of the five Decembrists who were hanged. In his famous 'Monument' Alexander Pushkin quite openly set his poetic creations against the acts of state and the victories of the Emperor Alexander, as though proclaiming the emergence in Russia of a new power, the power of the inspired word, more legitimate than the power of law and crown. It was not by chance that the poet Tyutchev called the assassin of Pushkin a 'regicide'.

In such circumstances young Dostoievsky could

not fail to understand that his enthusiasm for literature and his desire to become a creative artist were incompatible with service to the crown. Having entered the school of military engineers, following his father's wishes, he felt immediately that to his previous difficulties had been added the hard experience of drastically reduced freedom. Nevertheless, the years in which he served his first deprivation of freedom were of great importance for his mental stature. Acquaintance with exact science enabled him to realize the helplessness of rational knowledge in solving moral problems and spiritual enigmas. Here, in the Engineering College, he first rebelled against the unfounded claims of the 'Euclidean mind' and 'common sense'. 'For God's sake, why should I be concerned with the laws of nature and arithmetic, if for some reason I happen to dislike these laws and two by two?' exclaims the man 'from Underground' (*Notes, etc.*, Part I, III). These are the very sentiments Dostoievsky expressed in a letter to his father about his work at school: 'I cannot bear mathematics. What a peculiar science! And how stupid to study it. . . . Mathematics without application is just zero, and it has as much use as a bubble of soap' (5 May 1839). But in confessing his anti-scientific heresy to his father, he did not tell him, as he did to his brother Mikhail, of the great discoveries he made secretly in his independent quest into the depths of man's mind and his own heart.

His guides in these researches were the great creative minds of literature, both ancient and modern, English, German, and French, in addition to

Russian. Pushkin, Derzhavin, and Lomonosov find their rivals in Shakespeare, Schiller, Goethe, Victor Hugo, and, especially, Balzac. 'Balzac is great!' he tells his brother in a letter of 9 August 1838. 'His characters are the creation of the mind of a whole universe! Not the spirit of the age, but the probings of thousands of years have prepared such a culmination in a soul of a man.' Independently of Goethe, and as though by accident, he discovers the existence and meaning of a 'world literature'. From Homer to Balzac, all his predecessors in the search for truth about man, were poets in his eyes. And so he discovers the 'poet' within himself. He would have liked to join the world of poetry, not only the Russian, but the universal world and, what is most significant, poetry in his mind begins to merge with 'philosophy'. In the same year, 1838 (31 October), he writes to his brother: 'Philosophy should not be conceived as a simple mathematical equation in which the unknown is nature. Note, that a poet in a transport of inspiration is seeking God and consequently serves the purpose of philosophy. Consequently, poetic ecstasy is the ecstasy of philosophy. Consequently, philosophy is the same as poetry, only a higher degree of it!' On the basis of this and other similar enthusiastic declarations, one can say without exaggeration that in his eighteenth year Dostoievsky recognized within himself the artist and the thinker, 'the poet', and 'the philosopher'. At the same time the mystery of his own being began to acquire a religious character. Pascal becomes an important element in his development. He rapidly strides forward and soon overtakes his elder brother, his 'dearest Misha' who was studying engineering in nearby Reval and continued in every way to support Fyodor's faith in his predestination.

The words 'brother' and 'brotherhood' remained for ever sacred to Dostoievsky. He was infinitely grateful to his brother Mikhail for the moral support he received from him in his youth. He loved him tenderly, pitied him, and in turn tried to help him. After his return from Siberia he collaborated in the journal Mikhail was publishing, and after Mikhail's premature death in 1864, though himself hardly able to make ends meet, sacrificed everything to pay his brother's debts and to assist his indigent family. He preserved a lifelong deep feeling of gratitude also to the friend of his youth, I. N. Shidlovsky (1816–72), who inspired the kindred soul of young Dostoievsky with romantic enthusiasm for the ideals of literary creation accomplished in three dimensions simultaneously – artistic, philosophical, and religious. Schiller, E. T. A. Hoffmann, and Shakespeare became their common idols, and Shidlovsky himself grew in Dostoievsky's eyes to a 'beautiful and lofty creature, the right image of man presented to us by Shakespeare and Schiller'. (Letter of 1 January 1840.) Moreover, Shidlovsky could undoubtedly exercise much charm through his appearance. Although the two friends soon parted for ever and the tortuous path of Shidlovsky's life led him later to a monastic cell, Dostoievsky who liked to make fun of his own appearance contrasted it some decades later with the beautiful image of his elder friend. During the years of their close friendship, Dostoievsky finally made up his mind to dedicate himself to literary work. He awaited his 'liberation' with impatience and, not wishing to distress his father, carefully concealed from him the intention to begin 'writing' as soon as he had completed his education. The tragic death of his father at the hands of his outraged serfs (in June 1839) made the young Dostoievsky master of his future. Only three months later, in a letter to his brother (already quoted) he clearly defined that the purpose of his life was 'to solve the mystery of man'.

It has been suggested that the death of his father, instead of loosening young Dostoievsky's bonds, actually instilled in him for the rest of his life 'a sense of guilt' and imposed on all his works the mark of inconsolable grief. It is no mere accident, emphasizes Freud in his study of Dostoievsky, that the culminating achievement of his creation, *The Brothers Karamazov*, is a book about 'parricide' which, together with *Oedipus Rex* and *Hamlet*, must be counted among 'the three masterpieces of the literature of all time'. In accordance with his teaching, the father of psychoanalysis tried to interpret the strange convolutions of Dostoievsky's character and the main direction of his creative work by relating them to the early appearance of an 'Oedipus complex' and a 'neurosis' rooted in it: having from childhood onwards subconsciously desired his father's death and, therefore, feeling guilty of his terrible end, he tried to expiate his crime by self-torture, came to love suffering as just retribution and in his martyrdom found an inexhaustible source of inspiration. Contrary to the conviction of Dostoievsky and those around him that he suffered, at least since the years of his penal servitude, from epilepsy, Freud insists on his divergent 'posthumous' diagnosis. He explains the fits from which his 'patient' suffered until nearly the end of his life and other morbid manifestations of Dostoievsky's mysterious personality as an endless chain of neurotic experiments in self-flagellation. In Freud's opinion this 'masochism' is allied to Dostoievsky's 'sadism': his inclination to torture not only himself but others too, his readers in particular, as well as to his 'homosexual' leanings and 'gambling mania'. Consequently, we have before us either a bad case of an unhealed neurosis, or, at the worst, of an 'affective' epilepsy only, whose victim – a man of an 'enormous capacity for love which expressed itself in manifestations of super-human goodness' – inevitably became a 'sinner' and even a potential 'criminal'.

It is impossible in our time to ignore Freud, and his terminology has to be taken into account. However, it would not be out of place to observe here that had Freud ever written a psychoanalytical 'Life of Jesus', it could well be that the image presented would have been reminiscent of his portrait of Dostoievsky. Be that as it may, Freud himself recognizes that in the case of Dostoievsky 'before the problem of a creative artist, analysis must lay down its arms'. But then, of course, the question arises whether it is at all possible to grasp the 'personality' of Dostoievsky, if the inner meaning of his writings remains concealed and is used only as clinical material to confirm a preconceived and utterly impersonal analysis?

True, the death of his father was an important event in the life of Dostoievsky, but only for the reason that from then onwards there was no one on earth with whose will he had to comply in planning ahead. In this sense he became free. (Cf. letter to his brother of 19 July 1840.) But what should he have done with his freedom? Should he have submitted entirely to the will of the Heavenly Father and served God by his pen? If, at that time, he had cause to blame himself for anything, it was in the first place for his profound religious doubts. To get the feeling of the 'blank wall' which he faced in 1839, one has to read carefully the 'Necessary Explanation' by the eighteen-year-old Ippolit (*The Idiot*, Part 3, V–VII), saturated as it is with autobiographical material. Any biographer would have reason to assume that young Dostoievsky was then near to suicide. Thirty years later he invests the unhappy young Ippolit with his pen and his 'idea' that 'all that matters is life, life itself, the ceaseless everlasting process of discovering it, but not the discovery as such!' However, already then, thirty years before the creation of *The Idiot*, its future author might have felt that salvation was possible for him on condition that, disregarding himself for a time, he would venture to become a 'Columbus' not of a New World, but of the New Man who could find the way back to Christ. As to the suffering he himself endured through his 'craving to believe', this he recorded in his own name when he had reached his thirty-third year. (Letter to Natalia Fonvizina of February 1854.)

On leaving the Engineering College in 1843, he was transferred to the Corps of Military Engineers, but in the following year, against his guardian's advice, he relinquished his commission and took up writing as a profession. On the eve of 1845, the year he was enthusiastically initiated in his new service, not in that of the Empire, but of the People, the retired lieutenant Dostoievsky found himself face to face with life which attracted and frightened him by its majestic mystery.

In his unequal combat with it he hoped to find a measure of his own strength. By then he had already acquired some experience of life, including the ability to rule over 'subordinates'. (Cf. Ukaz on Discharge of 19 October 1844). But Dostoievsky was anxious to serve, not to command, and serving life, he was ready at first to surrender himself to all its whims and temptations. Possessing a modest income by inheritance, he started to plan all kinds of publishing enterprises and tried his luck in gambling; sensing the while his consuming 'Karamazov-like' voluptuousness, also part of his inheritance, he began to lead a dissolute life. Its echoes can be heard in *Notes from Underground*. But having stepped on to the road of sin, and tortured by his sinfulness, he tried to make up for it by strenuous work in using his pen to fight the evils of life, both without and within.

However, literary work, too, had its temptations no less dangerous to the moral equilibrium of the writer 'seeking after God' than the carnal ones.

29

Already in his first literary efforts, in the beginning of the 1840s, he saw himself in his dreams occupying a place in the world literature side by side, if not with Shakespeare, at least with Schiller. Egged on by an as yet unjustified 'ambition', he began to write dramas which he destroyed as soon as they were written. 'I have a terrible vice' – he wrote to his brother in 1846 – a 'boundlessly sensitive self-love and ambitiousness.' His proud dreams, nevertheless, had their limit. Thinking himself a 'poet', he never tried to compete with Pushkin or Lermontov and, once and for all, decided that he should refrain from writing poetry. Instead, he set himself with increased vigour to outdistance Gogol, then reigning supreme in Russian literature. He took a long time and great pains over his first book *Poor People*. When its manuscript at last reached Belinsky, this highest authority in progressive literary criticism of the day immediately proclaimed its author as a novelist who had overtaken Gogol. (Dostoievsky's letter of 1 February 1846.) For the first time Dostoievsky reached the goal he had set for himself: for the first time his faith in himself and his future received a brilliant confirmation. 'Am I really so great? I asked myself shamefacedly in timid exaltation. Do not laugh, I never afterwards thought I was great, but at the time . . .' (*A Writer's Diary*, 1877, 1. 'Old Memories'.) In short, the young writer was happy. But, in Pushkin's words, he was 'not created for happiness'.

All temptations lying in wait for those suddenly attaining fame set upon him. The proud ambition of

Dostoievsky quickly degenerated into easily wounded vanity, pretentious vainglory, and aggressive irritability. His fellow citizens in the singular republic of free Russian thinkers, with Belinsky at its head, began to wonder whether they had not overrated Dostoievsky; they demanded consistency. If, they argued, the essential meaning of the *Poor People* was that the poorest of the poor might be destined to be the first of the first, on condition that he was in truth 'a man' with human feelings of love and self-denial, then the upholder of such an ideal must live up to it. He must embrace the socialist faith in a society based on reason and renounce the ruling Christian obscurantism and hypocrisy. A clash between Dostoievsky and Belinsky, with his circle of prominent writers such as Nekrasov, Grigorovitch, and Turgenev, became inevitable. Whatever evil instincts were occasionally brewing in Dostoievsky's soul, he never ceased to cling to his own faith which knew no salvation for mankind other than through the veneration of the image of Christ.

The attitude to Belinsky, a difficult problem for Dostoievsky until the end of his life, was characteristic of the peculiar dialectic which generally determined his attitudes to individuals as well as to intellectual trends. This attitude usually began with a 'thesis', a positive affirmation, be it of a person or an idea, changing thereafter to an 'antithesis', to their sharp rejection, finally to culminate in a sort of 'synthesis' in which negation was oddly interlaced with the original impulse of affirmation. As to Vissarion Belinsky in particular, after a rapturous gratitude for the laurel wreath which he had bestowed on the unknown writer, Dostoievsky very soon became indignant with him for his 'atheism' and for allegedly 'reviling Christ' in Dostoievsky's presence. For a long time after the death of the 'tempestuous Vissarion', Dostoievsky revenged himself on him by abusing him in the vilest terms in private letters, all the while preserving warm feelings for him which came to the fore only at the end of the 1870s. (Cf. on the one hand, letters to the poet Maykov of 16 August 1867 and 18 February 1868, or to the critic N. N. Strakhov of 18 May 1871, and on the other, a letter to the widow of Belinsky of 5 January 1863, and references to him in *A Writer's Diary* of 1876, February 2, March 1, June 1 and 2.) A similar 'dialectical' oscillation can be traced in Dostoievsky's attitude to Gogol, Nekrasov, Turgenev, Victor Hugo, to members of his own family, to the women he loved, and also to the Russian Orthodox Church, to slavophilism and socialism. This was not due to superficial vascillating sentiments or thoughts, but on the contrary, to their basic complexity which harboured the possibility of developments in completely opposite directions. It may perhaps explain, why every new feeling which arose in Dostoievsky's heart was first of all a new source of torment.

It was no different with Dostoievsky's 'service' as a writer. It was based on his love for freedom of thought, freedom of speech, for his native tongue and its creator, the Russian people, and, what was perhaps most important, it was rooted in his predilection for hard work. Nonetheless, already in the first creative period, before his term of penal servitude, each one of his compositions had its particular 'history of illness', each one was born in pain. In the process of work, the initial attraction felt by the author towards his subject changed almost into disgust, and the satisfaction with the results achieved turned into complete disillusionment. This was already the case with *Poor People* and *The Double* – the first attempt by the author at a projection of his own duality; the same applies to *The Landlady* in which was delineated the life-plan of his friend Shidlovsky, or, more probably, the common task of both of them; this was true also of *White Nights*, the monument to his 'dreamy' romanticism and the idealism of his youth. On attaining its final form and breaking away in the process from the source of inspiration that gave it life, every creation of Dostoievsky became alien to him. He had no compunction to take his work to the literary market for sale like a piece of 'merchandise', a mere clot of energy spent in its production. The authors of *The Communist Manifesto* which had then appeared in the West would have had no difficulty in recognizing a true 'proletarian' in Dostoievsky. This attitude to his work remained unchanged until the very end: striving towards a complete comprehension and realization of the 'organic whole' of his elusive personality, he was bound to see even in his most outstanding creative successes only a faint allusion to his highest aim. Was he at all able to be incarnated within the limits of artistic creation?

It must be assumed that such doubts caused the

young writer to enter the field of political activity. The distinction between literature and 'politics' in Russia was, as is known, generally rather vague. The pen wielded in the service of the people could easily turn into a sword. True, such martial thoughts were far from Dostoievsky and his like-minded companions who, towards the end of the 1840s, had gathered round M. V. Butashevich-Petrashevsky, S. F. Durov, and N. A. Speshnev in resolute opposition to the ruling system. Still, they had preserved vivid memories of the Decembrists, the Russian revolutionaries of 1825, and were well abreast of intellectual trends and the great events in Western Europe connected with the historic date of 1848. At first they only discussed the programme of the hoped for liberation movement with the emancipation of the serfs as its foremost point, although the fight for freedom of speech through the establishment of a secret press was in the minds of some. The common source of their inspiration derived from the teachings of their elder contemporaries, the French utopian socialists: Saint-Simon, Fourier, Cabet. A few of them, and Dostoievsky in particular, greatly admired the genius of George Sand and her synthesis of socialism and Christianity. (Cf. *A Writer's Diary*, 1873, No. 50, and 1876, June, Chap. 1.) For the security police of Nicholas I, however, this was a sufficient ground for savage reprisals against Petrashevsky and his friends. Some members of the circle, Dostoievsky among them, were subjected to subtle torture: condemned to be shot, and taken to the scaffold for execution, they were told at the very

last moment that the death sentence had been commuted to penal servitude (22 December 1849). What
Dostoievsky experienced in that last minute, we
know from Prince Myshkin who speaks for Dostoievsky in terror and indignation. (*The Idiot*, I, Part
One, II: 'A greater torture than that the world knows
not.') There can be no doubt that the barb which
then entered Dostoievsky's heart remained there for
ever. This was the price he paid for the first period of
his service by his pen. The cruel sentence imposed on
Dostoievsky was as though by design connected
with the names of Gogol, his first 'rival' in the
literary sphere, and with that of Belinsky who had
conferred on him the title of a man of letters. Indeed,
Dostoievsky was condemned in particular for reading
to his circle of friends the forbidden essay by the late
Belinsky against Gogol, who had been led astray by
reactionary utopism. Two days after the mockery on
the scaffold, on Christmas eve, Dostoievsky in
shackles, together with other condemned, was sent
to Siberia for hard labour, and at the head of the
long procession on sledges there pressed forward a
'courier', perhaps the very same who twelve years
earlier so cruelly wounded the heart of young Fedya
on his way from Moscow to St. Petersburg. (Cf.
letter to his brother from Omsk of 22 February 1854.)

What penal servitude meant to Dostoievsky we
know first of all from his *Notes from the House of the
Dead*. He lived the entire four years in hell. What is
most striking, however, is not the fact that he survived the unspeakable torture, but that during all
that time he never for a moment ceased to live his

own life and in those terrible years continued on his own predestined path. After this experience he could never again doubt the benevolence of Providence. It was revealed to him already in his youth that 'fate can manifest the true will of Providence when it affects us with the irresistible power of our whole nature'. (Letter to his brother of 19 July 1840.) While in gaol at Omsk, he became fully convinced that his personal fate was dependent on the will of Providence. It was Providence that bestowed on him a fate of martyrdom and yet maintained his mind and heart immune in the midst of brigands and hangmen. It was Providence which endowed him with the strength meekly to endure the degrading humiliation; and with it instilled in his soul the sense of responsibility for all the evil reigning in the world and the readiness to bear the blame for it. This was the effect of 'the power of his whole nature'. 'Verily, everyone is guilty before all and for all' – this faith of Zosima's elder brother (*The Brothers Karamazov*, I, Part II, Book VI, IIa) was near to Dostoievsky even before the doors of the torture chamber had shut on him. The consciousness that the punishment he bore was merited – not just for the reading aloud of some essay – but merited for his personal original sin, could not fail to lighten the burden of his chains. Their ringing sounded in his ears like the echo of a purifying hymn. (Both before and after Dostoievsky there were not a few zealots in Russia who voluntarily bore heavy chains for the expiation of sins.)

But was Dostoievsky aware of any particular sinful act he had committed which demanded such a fierce purifying sacrifice? It would be appropriate at this point to touch on a question which has caused keen biographers so much painful perplexity. There is an assumption that 'Stavrogin's Confession' (a chapter from *The Possessed* originally rejected by the editor for obscenity) which contains the story of the assault on a little girl by Nicholas Stavrogin, is not an avowal of an imaginary character, but a confession of Dostoievsky himself. Regardless of all the arguments for and against such a supposition, two rather important circumstances should be stressed. According to Dostoievsky's text, Stavrogin not only corrupted his victim's innocence, but with a premeditated subtle design drove the child to suicide. In other words, Stavrogin's crime was not the rape of a minor or the violation of her childish innocence, but murder. And if that is so, who will suspect Dostoievsky of murdering an innocent child merely on the strength of a self-revelation by the prince of the 'devils'?

On the other hand, we have a highly significant though mysterious admission made by Dostoievsky in his own name. In remembering nearly twenty-five years later what he felt when, at the tsar's caprice, he was faced with 'inescapable' death, he remarks almost casually that 'in these last minutes . . . in the instinctive probing of oneself and the judging of one's life in a flash', he repented 'of some grave misdeeds the like of which every man conceals in his conscience all his life'. (*A Writer's Diary*, 1873, 50.) Is it likely that among the 'grave misdeeds' which all his life secretly burdened Dostoievsky's conscience there were crimes *à la Stavrogin* committed either before or

37

after his term in Siberia? Such a conjecture would ignore the fact that on the highly sensitive scales of Dostoievsky's conscience even the most ordinary human transgression often weighed as heavily as the spilling of blood, and evil intent no less than the premeditated deed of evil. 'I am often very sad,' he wrote to his wife from Moscow on 29 December 1866, 'as though I had committed a crime against someone.' His natural inclination to blame himself for any misfortune occurring around him is evidence of the acute sensitiveness of his conscience which incessantly tormented him. When his first-born child, three-months-old Sonya, died of pneumonia, he blamed himself for that too and wrote: 'All for my sins.' (Letter of 9 June 1868.) From such a point of view, he could well blame himself for the death of his father, and even more so for the death of his mother, and perhaps also for that of Pushkin. No two consciences are alike, and the individuality of Dostoievsky's deserves individual treatment.

Under such an incredibly heavy burden of conscience Dostoievsky was unable to find redemption even through the sufferings endured in penal servitude. Paradoxically, his physical and moral tortures perceived by him as deserved punishment, in healing the wounds of his conscience, deprived him, in so doing, of the main source of his inner torments and, dialectically, turned the healing process itself into a new punishment: for Dostoievsky was neither able nor wished to be free of torment. He discovered the martyr in himself and it grew upon him that he might through his own life reveal the meaning of martyr-

38

dom, or in the words of his 'Ridiculous Man': 'he knew sorrow and loved sorrow, he pined for torment and kept repeating that truth was attained only through torment.' Having left the nether world, he began somehow to regret the hell he lost, just as he regretted the lost paradise after his fall in Moscow. To his satisfaction, the infantry battalion in Semipalatinsk, in Siberia, to which he was transferred from prison as an officer reduced to ranks (1854) turned out to be only a purgatory from which there was an easy way back to Gehenna.

He very soon happened upon it. For the first time in his life the thirty-three-year-old Dostoievsky fell passionately in love. His chosen was Maria Isayeva – herself a sufferer, though not a sinless one. She admired the genius in a soldier's greatcoat, but did not reciprocate his love. When she was widowed, Dostoievsky married her, and her eight-year-old son, Paul ('Pasha'), became his son and with that was added a new source of most tormenting worry and anxiety for the rest of Dostoievsky's life. The story of Dostoievsky's first marriage which ends with Maria's death from consumption (1864) is the story of his first defeat in 'the fatal duel', in Tyutchev's phrase, between the sons of Adam and the daughters of Eve. 'Great is the gladness of love' – wrote Dostoievsky already in 1856 – 'but the sufferings are so awful that it were better never to love at all.' (Letter to Baron Wrangel from Semipalatinsk on 23 March 1856.) Love for Dostoievsky was a passionate yearning to overcome his own isolation. Before his term in prison he was hardly aware of it, and in any case he did not have much faith in a woman's mission to reunite a lonely 'dreamer' with reality. It was only in captivity that he came to understand clearly that, whether in fetters or free, he was virtually condemned to isolation, separated from the outside world by the barriers of his thought and fantasy. To overcome this inner confinement one had to see one's own self mirrored in another absolutely accepted personality, to see oneself through the eyes of another being, in short one had to love selflessly and be loved just as selflessly. Of necessity, therefore, all Dostoievsky's encounters with women – face to face and eye reflecting eye – had to end in tormenting disappointments.

To see Dostoievsky as he really was, vainly striving to find and accept himself, and really to love him, the chosen of his heart and mind would have had to become something like his double. Not just a second Dostoievsky, but a super-Dostoievsky, as it were. That was impossible. And after the Siberian Maria there were other 'Marias' and 'Marthas' to whom Dostoievsky gave his wildly agitated heart. But, in every case, the more intimate the relationship grew, the greater grew their indignation against the impossible task his loving anguish imposed on them. His ideal of love was not of this world. Adam found 'an help meet for him' in the Garden of Eden, but would he have found her after the banishment from Paradise? Longing for it everlastingly, Dostoievsky never came to know the harmonious accord of reciprocated love. He loved himself too little and too hesitatingly to inspire earthly women with love for him. Many years after his death he was repudiated even by his own daughter who was at birth given the name Lyubov ('Love').

While still in prison and, later, in the ranks at Semipalatinsk, and until his return to St. Petersburg by the grace of Alexander II in December 1859, Dostoievsky was obsessed with the idea that he was destined to live through a second youth, a 'better' youth in every sense than the first which was so abruptly broken off in 1849. He thought that he himself would be brighter, purer and nearer to the people whose high moral qualities were revealed to him in the most humiliated and rejected of its sons, his fellow sufferers. He dreamed also that his creations would be better, clearer, more perfect, that he would be able through them to share his growing knowledge of the human soul in perfect sincerity with himself and others. Severely condemning his proud isolation of the past, he rashly decided to rejuvenate himself by marriage. When it became evident that he had taken a false step, he made superhuman efforts to stifle his burning jealousy and to preserve his chivalrous feelings for his unfaithful wife.

His first steps in the literary sphere, newly re-opened to him, proved more successful. But here, too, he was not on firm ground at first. Dreaming of rejuvenation he unearthed the source of his erstwhile inspiration. He began to follow the precepts of the friend of his youth, the romantic Shidlovsky. While still in Semipalatinsk, he plunged into the study of the history of religions, including Islam, as well as into the study of philosophy. He read Kant and Hegel, became acquainted with the latest trends of thought in the West and planned not only to overtake Gogol, as in the period of the *Poor People*, but for ever to settle his accounts with the man whose clash with Belinsky had such dire consequences for Dostoievsky. And, indeed, among the writings of Dostoievsky's 'second youth' a prominent place, next to *The Insulted and Injured*, is taken by the tale, *The Village of Stepanchikovo*, in which Gogol is caricatured in the figure of Foma, i.e. Thomas, not one of the doubting Thomases, but as 'Foma Opiskin', i.e. Thomas the 'mis-speller'. In both books, pointers in opposite directions are easily discernible: back to the initial stage of the writer's service by his pen, and forward – from his 'second youth' to the concluding twenty years of life, when he almost succeeded in manifesting his 'boundless powers' in all their sweep, thus approaching fulfilment.

Not departing from his Siberian hopes of regaining his youth and of becoming a full and equal member of the young generation, Dostoievsky appeared in St. Petersburg on the eve of his fortieth year, like some Faust in search of his preordained Margaret. Through the bitter experience with his Siberian Maria, he knew that his innermost decision could have been prompted by the merciless Mephistopheles within himself. Nevertheless, he did not withstand the temptation to 'try his luck' in love. Time and again, with the characteristic ardour of a passionate gambler, he rushed heedlessly into the dangerous game whose stake was he himself. But who can tell?

Perhaps even then he craved for sweet torment above all.

How ill-starred he was in love stands out most tellingly in his relationship with Apollinaria Suslova (in the years 1861–67), the prototype of Pauline in his novel *The Gambler*. She was eighteen years younger than Dostoievsky and a convinced 'nihilist', a proud representative of that new generation into which he so much hoped to merge. In his close relations and quarrels with her the martyr discovered the tormentor within himself. As they say in Russia: 'Authority collided with authority.' The young woman who had already tasted the bitterness of suffering forthrightly exposed the sinister dialectic of compassion which inspired the author of *Notes from the House of the Dead* and *The Insulted and the Injured*. Without suffering there would be no cause for compassion; and consequently, concluded Dostoievsky's friend, treating him as her equal, in exalting his feelings of compassion he is greedily seeking and exploiting every manifestation of human martyrdom; he loves not only his own but also other people's sufferings; he depicts them with delight and even enjoys causing them, as for instance in his tormenting mistrustful love of her. Apollinaria's elder sister asked Dostoievsky point blank whether he 'liked to batten on other people's sorrows and tears', to which, deeply grieved, he replied: 'You saw me in my frankest moments and can, therefore, judge for yourself: whether I love to feast on other people's sorrows, whether I am gross (inwardly), whether I am cruel?' (Letter of 19 April 1865.) Though

43

grieved and trying to justify himself, Dostoievsky felt that, thanks to Suslova, he became aware of something dark in himself, hitherto concealed from his own understanding. In this sense she became a true 'help meet' to him; he was constantly drawn to her even before the death of his first wife in Moscow, and, indeed, after his second marriage. However, he no longer aroused either love or even pity in her, but only anger. (Something similar happened to Nietzsche in his encounter with Lou Salomé, the representative of the next generation of intrepid Russian women.)

But Faust would not give in. Dostoievsky became for a time 'The Knight of the sorrowful countenance', as it were. He wandered about abroad in search of forgetfulness and of new torments in gaming houses; simultaneously he collaborated in the journals of his brother Mikhail, disclosing the secrets of his first dissolute youth in the *Notes from Underground*. But even in this period, covering the creation of his artistic masterpiece, *Crime and Punishment*, living as he did in severely straitened circumstances and suffering from more frequent attacks of his 'holy sickness', he never gave up the dream of at last finding his promised Margaret. The twenty-year-old girls to whom in that period he offered his heart or his hand, or both, were about twenty-five years younger than he: Anna Korvin-Krukovskaya was born in 1847; Sofya Ivanova, his own niece whom he loved ardently to the end of his days 'as a sister and a daughter', or rather as Dante loved Beatrice, was born in 1846. In 1846, too, was born Anna Snitkina, who in 1867

44

became his second wife. Is it a chance coincidence that 1846 is also the year of the appearance of Dostoievsky's literary first-born – the *Poor People*?

Dostoievsky's biographers describe his second marriage as 'happy'. Did it, however, put an end to his martyrdom? Is it, indeed, possible to imagine that a martyr should live 'in married bliss'? A careful confrontation of all known facts clearly contradicts the complacent valuation of Fyodor Mikhailovich's marriage to 'Anya'. After his marriage, too, he never ceased to cherish the ideal image of Margaret, which had become unattainable to him in reality. The second marriage of Dostoievsky was a marriage of convenience for both sides, if not in its coarse sense, in a deeper sense it was 'advantageous' to both. Though only in an abstract form, the youth and innocence of Anya satisfied the basic demands of his tormented heart. But he was under no delusion that he might find in her gaze his higher, yet to be incarnated, self, as he had dreamed was possible in his tenderly rapturous love for his Beatrice-Sofya. Neither did Anya become the judge of his conscience or of his creations, as Apollinaria could well have done. She was and remained till the end an uncritical admirer of his artistic talents, his nurse, his secretary, the shrewd manager of his affairs, and finally even his publisher. However, that she became the mother of his children was more important to him than all else. This was Dostoievsky's paramount 'advantage'; while her 'advantage' consisted first of all in that she became the wife of a 'great man', even if, as we know, he never considered himself as 'great'.

From the beginning all this unavoidably turned into a new source of suffering for Dostoievsky. His sense of loneliness was deepened and he was overcome by a feeling of guilt for the inadequacy of his love. He tried to atone for his guilt by constantly whipping up his passion and was infinitely grateful to his wife for making him a father. But paternity became in turn a tormenting passion. The shortest separation from his family intensified his longing for them and caused a painful anxiety for the fragile well-being of the children and his wife. This anxiety often took the form of nightmarish dreams. He was constantly pursued by fear that the children may have to atone for the sins of the father. When towards the end of his life, his last child, Alyosha, died suddenly from an epileptic fit, Dostoievsky saw in this manifestation of the laws of heredity a new proof of his guilt before his children. He went immediately to the cloister of the Elder Ambrosius to seek consolation in his grief (June 1878). Although Dostoievsky did not identify his Christian creed with the tenets of the established Russian Orthodox Church even in the last period of his life, he readily performed its rites and ceremonies for the sake of his wife and children, and in the fulness of his feelings not infrequently knelt with them in prayer.

His marked turn towards the Church was explained by Dostoievsky himself by the fact that over the course of the years he began to feel more and more Russian. Unable to overcome his isolation in personal relationships, he all the more persistently tried to achieve communion with the supra-personal whole: with the Russian people and all it held holy. His thought and his imagination were working towards this end. Without this craving he would hardly have attained that degree of self-revelation to which he rose as artist and thinker from the middle of the 1860s onwards.

Already during his first journey to the West at the beginning of that period and, later, when he sought refuge there from the implacable creditors of his brother (1867–71), he formed the conviction that humanity unfaithful to Christ needed a new liberating word which could only be proclaimed by the all-suffering Russian people continuing in the path of Christ. But who was called to speak in its name? The dilemma he faced was either to hold his peace for ever or to take upon himself in all humility the urgent Herculean task. It is precisely to this end that from then onwards all his writings, artistic or other, such as *A Writer's Diary* (1873–80), were dedicated. Accordingly, the service by his pen was never as tormenting for Dostoievsky as in the concluding period of his creative life. In all his creations – from *Crime and Punishment* to *The Brothers Karamazov* and his Pushkin speech – he strove, not disdaining the guise of an entertaining novelist, to reveal himself not as an advocate of an already accepted doctrine, but as the precursor of 'The New Man' and 'The New Word', as a seer of things to come. How could he, with such a design in mind, find the least gratification in the results of his efforts? He toiled and suffered agony in the foreboding, which seized him already

47

while he was writing *The Idiot*, that within ten years death would silence him mid-way.

All the vicissitudes which turned Dostoievsky's life into an endless chain of painful ordeals – illness, poverty, hard labour, banishment, reverses in love, failure to be recognized in literature, and above all his own 'unbearable character' – could not break the spirit of the martyr, nor deflect him from his life's course. Every new trial enriched his personality, and with its growing complexity grew the conviction that he would finally succeed in conquering all the evil spirits within himself. In the very last years of his life, his growing spiritual stature became evident even to the world at large. The younger generation began to surround him with love and to heed his word. In this he was again helped by Pushkin, the guardian angel of his early years. There were moments during public readings by Dostoievsky when, in reciting Pushkin's poetry, he identified himself with the poet to such an extent that the close indissoluble bond between them became almost tangible. But Dostoievsky was able to send all around him into real transports of ecstasy in reciting the poem in which Pushkin identified himself, as it were, with the prophets of the Bible. Then – relates a contemporary – 'with his weak voice which by some miracle could be heard in the farthest corners of the large hall, Dostoievsky pierced your very heart. . . .' The thought was born and grew that Russia was graced with a Prophet of her own.

II

The Artist

To attain perfection one must first be puzzled by
many things.

The Idiot, II, Chapter 7

In our day Dostoievsky is almost universally recognized as one of the outstanding masters of literary
art, by whose creations world literature has gained
in scope and depth. Yet this recognition was slow
to mature. Even decades after his death it appeared
unlikely that posthumous fame might adorn Dostoievsky's name with a halo of immortality. In his
own lifetime most of the representative Russian
critics and authors, including Tolstoy, were inclined
to think that Dostoievsky's works would hardly
outlive their author – a view not unlike Dostoievsky's
own.

Today, nearly a hundred years since the emergence
of Dostoievsky's masterpieces, when their fate has
become intertwined with the destiny of world
literature as a whole and no more depends either on
the further evolution of Russian letters or even on
the future of the Russian language, it is easier to
understand, and to forgive, the shortsightedness of
the past. For it is actually the misjudged himself who
must take the main responsibility for the misjudgment
of the 19th century.

In the process of undermining the then generally

accepted literary canons and forms, Dostoievsky realized only towards the end of his life that his mission was to proclaim his 'own word' not merely as a thinker but also as an artist. So long as his particular task in literary art remained unrevealed to himself, or more precisely, so long as he had not fully succeeded in expressing his original aesthetic message through the medium of his artistic works, these implicitly reflected the hesitations of their author between faithfulness to literary tradition and his rebellion against it. Thus the view gained ground, and prevailed upon Dostoievsky himself, that he was lacking in force to cope with his artistic designs. It is only now, in the light of the subsequent evolution of world literature, that we can clearly see the source of the artistic 'errors' and the alleged 'weakness' of Dostoievsky's talent; they testified to his irrepressible instinctive endeavour to transform the language of poetic imagination into a new mightier tool of the human will and spirit.

This endeavour of Dostoievsky the artist is discernible above all in his treatment of the conventional form of the novel (in Russian: *roman*). Up to this day, Dostoievsky is mostly accepted as a novelist of genius. Nonetheless, more than one distinguished arbiter of literary taste puts aside some bulky tome of Dostoievsky's, e.g. a volume of *The Brothers Karamazov*, wondering whether this 'novel' would not gain in artistic quality if it were less complex in its composition and considerably reduced in size. But is his last great work really a novel in the conventional sense? True, the description is the author's.

However, an objective study of his artistic evolution must suggest that such a definition was no more than a semi-ironical concession to current terminology, if not a deliberate adaptation to the requirements of the book-trade. In 1875, in the 'Conclusion' of the last but one of his great 'novels' written in the form of memoirs of a 'raw youth', Dostoievsky drew a dividing line between himself and the 'novelists' of his time, Tolstoy in particular.

The critical appraisal of this book included in its last chapter, emphasizes that it should not, properly speaking, be regarded as a 'novel'. Disguised as a fictitious reviewer of his own work, Dostoievsky explains that the prerequisite of a novel was the real existence of 'beautiful, accomplished forms' of everyday life, and, first and foremost, of a firmly established family order whose beauty was based on the bedrock of 'honour and duty'. Yet all this, the 'reviewer' goes on to tell us, was a thing of the past in Russia. The old order with its characteristic 'saga of the Russian home', in Pushkin's phrase, was about to wither away. With the disintegration of Russia's gentry, there was everywhere but flotsam and jetsam, 'flying splinters, litter and dust', that is to say, material utterly useless to a novel builder. That is why a Russian novelist worthy of the name had no other choice in this period of transition but to turn to the 'historical genre'. This was exactly what the author of *Anna Karenina* was doing, even when he tried to mirror his own time. (Cf. the analysis of Tolstoy's 'historical novels' in *A Writer's Diary*, 1877, July–August.) Where then should a writer cast his eye, if he was well alive to the fact that the old established Russian families 'were in rapidly increasing numbers acquiring the character of accidental families which were absorbing the former amidst the general confusion and chaos', as exemplified by the house of Versilov, the father of the 'raw youth'? – 'I confess' – exclaims the author – 'I wouldn't wish to be the novelist of an accidental family! The work is unrewarding and without beauty. At all events, all characters in question are still in flux and therefore not fit for an artistically accomplished representation. Grave errors might occur, exaggerations, oversights. In any case, one would have to rely too much on guesswork. Well, what is then left to a writer who does not wish to restrict himself to the historical genre and who is obsessed by longing for that which is in flux? – To guess and . . . to err.'

It is now understandable why Dostoievsky was bound to discover 'grave errors, exaggerations and oversights' also in his two preceding 'novels', *The Idiot* and *The Possessed*, which, as can be seen from his letters to his friends, made him extremely unhappy. As to *The Brothers Karamazov*, here the author deliberately focused the narrative on a family foredoomed by its 'accidental' character to self-destruction. All this shows that in the course of his artistic self-fulfilment it gradually dawned on Dostoievsky that he was facing the alternative either to cling to the accepted form of the novel and to forgo the projection of his chaotic age into literature, or to testify in the idiom of art to his 'time of trouble' and to reconcile himself to the reputation of a hapless novel writer. His choice was made, though rather inadvertently, already at the time of the creation of *Crime and Punishment,* and even earlier, when the *Notes from Underground* were conceived.

Turning once more to Dostoievsky's afterthoughts at the end of *The Raw Youth*, one is justified in saying, paradoxical as this may sound, that his last five great books are novels about the 'impossibility of the Russian novel in the future'. Did this apply only to the 'novel' and exclusively to the 'Russian' one? For the answer to this question Dostoievsky the thinker was not less responsible than Dostoievsky the artist.

However, Dostoievsky made light not only of his title as a 'novelist' but even hesitated to recognize an 'artist' in himself. Most significant in this respect is his letter from Dresden (of the 9/21 October 1870) addressed to the poet A. N. Maykov, which is full of complaints about the difficulties he was meeting in composing *The Possessed*: 'Generally speaking' – he wrote – 'there is nothing in the world more repulsive to me than literary work, i.e. my own writing of novels and stories.' Then, after a brief exposition of the theme of the new book he was writing, he goes on: 'There is not the slightest doubt that it will be bad; rather a poet than an artist, I have always chosen themes beyond my grasp. That is why I shall spoil it, for certain. The theme is too strong. Still, as no one of the critics who have judged me has denied till now that there was some talent in me, it is probable that this lengthy novel too will not be altogether bad in places. Well, that is all.' – 'All', indeed? – Only, if one is clear about the distinction

Dostoievsky made between the 'artist' and the 'poet' and his aesthetics in general.

Who is a real 'artist' according to Dostoievsky? In the first place the painter: Raphael, Holbein, Claude Lorraine. Only a writer blessed with the creative power akin to theirs to conjure up by means of the written word well balanced colourful paintings full of life, in which every detail was organically related to the composition of the whole, while the whole stood out as an independent living entity, only he and he alone would deserve the admiration due to a true master. Such an artist of the pen was, of course, Pushkin. Every one of his short stories was in this sense a masterpiece: they were not products of playful fancy, nor fables with a moral, nor imitations of life, but life itself, an everlasting source of revelation to the human soul. Citing Pushkin's *Queen of Spades* an an example which bridged, as it were, the gap between common experience and the 'other world', Dostoievsky concluded his comment enthusiastically: 'That is art, indeed!' (Letter of 15 June 1880.) But to achieve the union of poet and painter in his own work appeared to him a hardly attainable goal.

Recalling a conversation he once had with Belinsky about the dangers inherent in the poetical gift, Dostoievsky pointed out that 'poetry was, so to speak, the inner fire of talent'; whoever was endowed with talent had in him at least a spark of poetry, and be he only a tradesman (*A Writer's Diary*, 1876, February, 2). 'Talent', in turn, was always identified by Dostoievsky with spontaneous originality of the intellectual and emotional reaction to one's experience (cf., for instance, the introductory remarks in *The Idiot*, III, 1). Well aware since his early youth of his own originality and, consequently, of his own literary talent, he was certain that his writings were inspired by the inner glow of poetry. But was that enough to evaluate them as something approaching artistic perfection? A stern judge of his own achievements, he preferred to claim for his 'novels' no higher a title than that of 'poems', i.e. of a literary form which in his terminology did not demand from the author superb mastery of composition and plastic presentation. On the other hand, attributing to himself the dignity of a 'poet', he was most generous in recognizing the 'poetical' quality of the work of many of his contemporaries; not only of Tolstoy's 'historical novels', but also of the plays of Ostrovsky, and even of some of Belinsky's writings.

In 1874 Dostoievsky summarized his basic conception of the relationship between the 'poet' and the 'artist' in literature in this short note: 'To write a novel, one has first of all to provide oneself with one or more strong impressions actually experienced by the author's heart. That is the task of the poet. Such an impression brings forth the theme, the plan, a well balanced whole. But at this point the artist has to take over, though the artist and the poet help one another in both cases.' These somewhat nebulous formulae find their clarification in Dostoievsky's correspondence of the same period. In one of his letters to the philosopher N. N. Strakhov he stated: 'Ignoring my limitations, carried away by poetical transport, I undertake to express an artistic idea which I cannot master'; in consequence 'several different novels and stories are squeezed into one, and so there is no measure, no harmony.' (Letter from Dresden of 5 May 1871.) But was Dostoievsky's self-evaluation fair? Was he really obliged, as he and his critics supposed, to write to measure and to create in consonance with the established rules of harmony? – In the end, as shown, he discovered that he was not.

Already at an earlier stage, when he formulated his aesthetical principles, he had prepared the ground for his vindication as an artist in the face of accepted yardsticks and rules. In an essay *About Art*, published in 1861 in his brother's review *Vremya* (*Time*), Dostoievsky emphasized that his repudiation of the *l'Art pour l'Art* theory did not imply acquiescence in a narrow-minded utilitarianism. It was true that art served life and fulfilled a most useful function in the evolution of the human kind, but this usefulness was not immediately recognizable; there was no reliable scale which could indicate whether and to what extent some single work of art might be useful or useless. Its true value must therefore be assessed on the strength of its intrinsic merits. These, however, were determined by the intensity with which contemporary real life was encompassed through the specific art medium. 'Art' – states Dostoievsky categorically – 'is always contemporaneous and realistic, it never existed differently and, what is more, it cannot exist differently.' But the contemporary reality to be reflected in a work of art was by no means an indiscriminate accumulation of things and happenings coeval with the artist; for the real essence of 'reality' at any stage of historical existence were the tensions and tendencies, the strivings and purposes, the ends and ideals of the period concerned. Human existence was actually an incessant projection into anticipated future which though 'endless, ever alluring and new has nevertheless its own *akme*', so that 'life itself was nothing else but the everlasting search for this highest point'. Its name was timeless perfection. In aspiring in its own domain to the revelation of 'beauty', of perfect harmony, over which 'time has no sway any more', art throughout the ages testified that the highest goals of man were not unattainable. And to bear witness to that, according to Dostoievsky, was precisely the task of Russian literature in his own time.

In delineating the tasks of art in general and of contemporary Russian literature in particular, Dostoievsky actually drew up in the essay of 1861 a working programme for the concluding stage of his self-fulfilment. 'The more one is in dissonance with surrounding life, in disharmony, in struggle' – he wrote – 'the stronger the longing for beauty'; Russia of his day, he thought, was going through 'a time of most intensive life', for it was 'essentially a time of urgency, of strife, of uncertainty and of faith'. Therefore, it was incumbent on Russian literature to give adequate expression to the turmoil of the age, thus helping modern man in his search for a final goal. 'But how' – he asked himself – 'could one really define clearly and convincingly what exactly ought to be done in order that the ideal of all our wishes and of all that the whole of humanity desired and aspired to should be attained? One can guess, invent, surmise, explore, dream, and narrate, but it is impossible to compute beforehand every future step of the whole of mankind as if it were something in a calendar.' All the more so as this was true also of the past: 'Here, too, we are not able to set up a calendar, and history cannot yet be regarded as an exact science' (in Russian *naóoka*, in the sense of the French *science* or the German *Wissenschaft*).

Dostoievsky's programme of 1861 obviously anticipated his epigram, so to speak, concerning the 'novel' of 1875. The earlier account of what he perceived as his literary mission appears, however, more comprehensive than the latter one. While this was confined to one specific aspect of the literary form he had made his own, the essay of 1861 indicated that he visualised his artistic activity merely as a means to an end of a meta-aesthetical significance. Indeed, the art he aspired to since the beginning of the 1860s had been conceived by him as a subtle instrument of human knowledge, destined to probe the mysteries of historical existence beyond the reach of purely theoretical, conceptual exploration. In this ambitious conception the artist and the thinker in Dostoievsky merged into one.

The concentration of Dostoievsky's mind on the twin task of inventing and revealing in the same breath, as it were, by means of intellectual imagination or, more precisely, of visionary thought was not the result of sudden inspiration. Already as a young man, still groping in the dark in search of an original form of self-expression, the idea crossed his mind that his literary work might become the mould of a new synthesis between metaphysical thought and artistic vision, between abstract speculation and concrete representation, in short, between 'science', in the Russian meaning of the term, and art. It is his *alter ego*, Vassily Mikhailovitch Ordynov, the main character in *The Landlady* of 1847 (modelled perhaps on the image of his friend Shidlovsky) who first broaches the bold intention. 'He was devoured' – the author tells us – 'by the deepest, the most insatiable passion which consumes one's whole life. . . . This passion was – science.' And he goes on to explain: 'In his mind gradually emerged an image of an idea, still veiled and vague, yet marvellously elating, embodied in a new resplendent form, which tormented his soul urging for release; though still timidly, he felt its originality, its truth, and its peculiarity; creativeness already responded to his abilities; it took shape and gained strength. But the time of materialization and building was still far away, perhaps very much so, perhaps impossible altogether' (*The Landlady*, Part 1, I).

Overlaid by episodes of an ill-starred story, already rejected by Belinsky as 'neuropathic nonsense', Dostoievsky's programmatic exposition of his innermost intentions as artist and thinker remained unnoticed; and yet these accidental formulations pointed not only to the original form but even to the content of the author's future work. This is what he had to relate further about his twin brother, Ordynov: 'Everything arose before him in colossal forms and imagery. . . . He saw whole cities built and destroyed

59

in his very sight . . . how whole races and peoples appeared, grew and withered away. . . . Every thought, every impalpable dream attained embodiment almost at the moment of conception. . . . He was thinking not in ethereal ideas but in whole worlds, in whole creations.' Out of this came the sketch of a work concerning Church history, 'and his warmest, most ardent convictions flowed from his pen'. And the narrator speculates: 'Perhaps a whole original, self-existent idea would find realisation in him. Perhaps his destiny was to be an artist in science' (*ibid.*, Part 2, III).

In correlation with Dostoievsky's lifework, there can hardly be any doubt that the 'science' in which he as a young man dreamt to excel was primarily philosophy of universal history accounting for the emergence, decline and fall of nations and empires, and that from the outset he considered imaginative art as the most serviceable tool for the penetration of this mystery to which the history of religion might contain the clue. True, at first sight any one of Dostoievsky's great books appears to be very remote from any kind of 'science', be it plain history or its metaphysical interpretation. Taken together, however, they reveal themselves as a deliberate attempt to attack one and the same problem from many directions – that concerning the meaning of historical life as it was seen from Russia in Dostoievsky's time. The problem was in essence a theoretical, a philosophical one; but rooted in a reality defined by Dostoievsky in his postscript to *The Raw Youth* as history in the melting pot, it suggested a new elastic method of approach and exposition, in which 'scientific' disquisition had to be subordinated to artistic divination. It was this basic conception which informed Dostoievsky's style in the broader sense. All 'digressions' in his 'novels' directly or indirectly relating to Russian, European or universal history must, therefore, be recognized as an integral element of the artistic composition concerned. Remembering how often these 'digressions' have a bearing on Church history, one will easily agree that they are all best represented by Ivan Karamazov's 'Legend of the Grand Inquisitor' which looks most remarkably as though it were the consummation of Ordynov's erstwhile dreams and could be eliminated from the narrative only together with Ivan Karamazov himself.

Here we are at the point from which it can be clearly seen how Dostoievsky's style in the wider sense is reflected in his singular artistic means and devices. To wed philosophical thought to imagined reality he had to conceive a medium in which both would appear organically correlated. He discovered it by constructing a world of his own populated by thinkers, each with his specific articulate philosophy.

The world of Dostoievsky thus resembles, surprising as this may appear, that of Plato in whose Dialogues the 'Elder' Socrates and his disciples are constantly involved in the exploration of problems vital for their time and for the ultimate destiny of Hellenic culture. Other than Plato, however, in whom the artist was superseded by the philosopher, his distant Russian descendant contrived to establish a balance of the two powers which concurred in the process of his self-realization and incorporated the philosophical controversy into the wider sphere of poetical epos. In this way he obtained the possibility of endowing abstract ideas and systems with the quality of concrete life and, simultaneously, of creating images of living human beings whose fate derived from their respective ideas and systems. The clash between these individual embodiments of conflicting philosophies is the core of Dostoievsky's tragic epos; their actions bring to life the last consequences of their fateful philosophical obsessions, while in the background of their common environment hovers the ever present crucial problem as to what is going to happen to Russia and to the whole Christian civilization if events of the kind depicted by Dostoievsky's narrators will take their course uncomprehended and uncontrolled.

On the face of it, a book like *Crime and Punishment*, artistically, no doubt, the most perfect among Dosstoievsky's 'novels', can be read and enjoyed as a thriller, the annoying 'digressions' notwithstanding. Yet, one has to remember that Dostoievsky's literary taste had been nurtured on Biblical stories which can and should be read on different levels – from that of the wise and enlightened down to that of the nursery. Of similar nature is the detailed account of how the student Rodion Raskolnikov, son of a pious mother and brother of a proud girl, came to commit premeditated murder with robbery, and in the end, prompted by the Holy Writ, admitted his guilt, was condemned to penal servitude and accepted suffering as a means of purification. However, if that were the whole story, its author would rank, despite his sublime mastery in creating tension, his subtlety of detail and his exceptional power in stirring the reader's emotional reaction, as one of the great novelists of the 19th century, of the stature of a Victor Hugo or of Charles Dickens, but he would not represent a class by himself. But Raskolnikov is not akin to any of their central characters. He is not of the same substance even which characterizes Tolstoy's Pierre Bezukhov or Konstantin Levin; the murder deliberately committed by him is not just a specimen of the crime so defined; consequently, the whole story is far from a fable on a colossal scale with a Christian moral meaning in it. Dostoievsky's *Crime and Punishment* is, in fact, his exposure of the deadly consequences inherent in modern individualism based on Positivism, and Raskolnikov is the exponent of this anti-religious philosophy, obsessed by the demonic ambition of making its theoretical and practical ends meet. The rest is catastrophe.

We well remember that Raskolnikov is the author of an essay which actually led to his downfall. This is one of Dostoievsky's devices designed to unfold before the mind's eye the intricate interplay of theory and practice in life as much as in his own art. Many other outstanding figures in the world of Dostoievsky are, like Raskolnikov, writers, constructors of philosophical systems or inventors of original historical conceptions, and all of them live up to their 'original idea' or die as its voluntary victims. Such are Svidrigaylov (also in *Crime and Punishment*), Prince

Myshkin (in *The Idiot*), Shatov, Kirillov, and Stavrogin (in *The Possessed*) and, above all, the four brothers Karamazov together with their father. Incidentally, two of the four are also writers: not only Ivan but even young Alyosha who composed the 'Life' of the Elder Zosima; their brother Mitya, therefore, had good reason to proclaim: 'The Karamazovs are not scoundrels but philosophers, because all genuine Russians are philosophers' (*The Brothers Karamazov*, Book XI, IV). All relations of these 'philosophers' with the world outside, all their intellectual and emotional reactions to it, including other human beings, are determined by their creator's fundamental equation: man = idea. They face us not as theorizing individuals but as personified ideas in action, or to use the French philosophical term, as *idées-forces*. In other words, their intellectual energy is not a part aspect of their natural psychological outfit, as with other novelists of the period, but, on the contrary, their psychological life appears entirely adapted and subordinated to a fixed idea, as it were. In that sense, the whole world of Dostoievsky can be described as one vast laboratory of experimental philosophy.

And yet it is a 'world' within the meaning of realistic art, not a phantastic cluster of nebulae inhabited by phantoms. What then are the foundations on which Dostoievsky's art has erected it?

These seem to be the technical devices applied by the architect.

In the first place, and in line with the theory expounded in 1861, Dostoievsky assumed the posture of a chronographer of his own time. All the strange and sinister happenings related in his great books take place in the reign of Tsar Alexander II and are well and soundly set within this chronological frame. The colour of time and place is meticulously preserved. In fact, Dostoievsky constantly pursued his endeavour to remain 'true to life'; before placing a plot in a specific setting, e.g. in a monastery, he used painstakingly to study the scene of the visualized events. New and perturbing as the interaction of ideas contemplated by Dostoievsky the thinker might have been, as an artist professing adherence to realism, though 'in a higher sense', he was always anxious to implant the new into old familiar ground. The personification of modern individualism ready to override all moral inhibitions, in *Crime and Punishment*, might have failed to produce its realistic effect, were Raskolnikov, this unfortunate forerunner of the Russian brand of Bonapartism, not so skilfully confronted with his subtle antagonist, the exponent of old-established Law and Order, Porfiriy Petrovich, the investigator of both the crime and the criminal idea behind it.

A further means of enhancing the realistic effect of the dramatized encounters between personified ideas was found by Dostoievsky in the distinction he forcefully underlined between himself as author and the various narrators in his books. This was, of course, an old invention applied long before Dostoievsky of which he made use already in *Poor People*, cast in the form of an exchange of letters. Later on, however, he apparently hesitated between the conventional technique of identifying himself with an omniscient narrator and the other possibility of intimating to the reader that the author conveyed to him someone else's testimony. While *Crime and Punishment* is composed in accordance with the technique of omniscience and comes in general nearest to the common type of novel, any of the later great books of Dostoievsky's each in turn introduces its own reporting chronicler supplanting his account of events with a running commentary; sometimes, notably in *The Possessed*, the commentator emerges under the guise of a distinct character playing a part in the events themselves. By placing between himself and the 'cases' related a shadow author without name and fame, often to the detriment of the composition, Dostoievsky pursued a dual purpose: first, to divest the figments of his speculative imagination of their fictitious character, and secondly, to obtain the necessary scope for embroidering the narrative with observations, often tendered in the form of a hypothetical interpretation by witnesses sworn in, as it were, as unbiased observers. By this means the narratives have each been provided with an individual frame within which the plot unfolds before the reader as if he were seeing it through the eyes of the narrator from the inside of the story. He, the quasi-independent narrator, is always there to testify again and again that this is no fiction, that it is real life itself. Adding thus a new dimension to the projections of his artistic imagination, Dostoievsky reinforced their realistic texture and made the greater part of his last books to appear as a series of reports on actual *causes célèbres*.

66

However, there was only one cause which inspired Dostoievsky both as artist and thinker. This was, as already mentioned, the fate and future of Christian civilization. Like Ordynov, the hero of his youth, he was engrossed in the contemplation of 'whole worlds', of 'whole creations', faithful to his ideal to fulfil himself as 'an artist in science', or more precisely, as an artist in Moral Philosophy based on a comprehensive Philosophy of History. It is impossible to form an adequate idea of Dostoievsky's original art unless one is guided by a synopsis of his life's work. Its unique and unalterable object was the tracing of a path out of the moral and spiritual labyrinth of the time by throwing into sharp relief its evils and aberrations and by contrasting them with the less conspicuous but not less real promises of salvation inherent in man.

Untimely death prevented Dostoievsky from crowning his work with an all-embracing composition which he had contemplated and which might also have provided a clue to the solution of the great problem of his artistic conscience: how to overcome the difficulties of realistically designing the life of a 'positively good man'. Indeed, whenever Dostoievsky tried to perform this task he inevitably failed. The saintly 'idiot' becomes an accessory before the event in a case of murder and in the end is engulfed by the darkness from which he had emerged; similarly, the insight of the wise Elder Zosima does not help him to prevent the murder of old Karamazov; and as to his disciple Alyosha, we are left guessing what might have happened to him later on in the lowlands of the secular world. For Dostoievsky's crowning work, the sequel to his last great book, remained unwritten. He obviously was right in assuming that a harmonious composition was not in line with his artistic disposition and mission.

In consequence, the pulse of real life which becomes perceptible through Dostoievsky's literary work is that of a world throbbing on the verge of despair because its very heart was, according to his intuition, gravely ill. His imagination was permanently fastened on this one and indivisible reality: on a world without stability, in the throes of utter spiritual confusion, exposed to the danger of collective insanity, and yet unaware of the perils ahead. Faced with this ultimate reality, Dostoievsky the artist, not less than Dostoievsky the thinker, felt impelled to assume the part of the time's healer. His books, framed as separate chronicles showing from different angles the various aspects of the time of trouble, can be read therefore also as reports of an early pioneer of social psychiatry. It is not by accident that so many inhabitants of Dostoievsky's world are clearly defined as mental cases, while the author left it to his 'reporters' to wonder regarding others (e.g. Nastasya Filipovna in *The Idiot* or Stavrogin in *The Possessed*) whether their outward behaviour could not best be explained by fits of madness. This, too, is one of the devices Dostoievsky employed to enhance the impression that the world of his making was not an imaginary one, but as real as common sense might wish it to be. Still, the plain fact that madness appeared endemic in this world implicitly suggested that abnormality was a sign of the age, that it was symptomatic for a time 'out of joint'.

With concrete historical reality in the background, Dostoievsky secured the possibility unobtrusively to blend the concrete with the abstract and created a whole gallery of realistically individualized human beings embodying a great variety of obnoxious philosophies. True, the passionate and enraged Rogozhin (in *The Idiot*), the killer next to Raskolnikov in the chronological order of Dostoievsky's creations, is not burdened with the gift of articulate thinking, but he is actually merely the antagonist of the dispassionate 'humble knight' Myshkin and is charged by the author with the task of exposing the deadly dangers inherent in the good and the beautiful when they are cursed with impotence and divorced from resolute action. In this remarkable case Dostoievsky was compelled by his realism to betray his most cherished ideal and to reconcile himself, admitting failure, to a blurred outline of the personified idea of good. All the more impressive were his artistic attacks on ideas which to him exemplified the essence of evil: in the same way that egocentric individualism appeared unmasked in the image of Raskolnikov, Stavrogin's image, an embodiment of willpower for its own sake, was a stern warning against the voluntarism of the new age which, not guided by a moral ideal, must needs degenerate in an empty anti-intellectualism culminating in suicidal scepticism. Side by side with Stavrogin, other 'possessed' men embody the ideas of extreme atheism combined with the deification of man (Kirillov), of power-worship

(Verkhovensky junior), of irresponsible romanticism (Verkhovensky senior), of heathen tribal nationalism (Shatov) or of egalitarianism gone mad (Shigalyov). To find one's way among all these and similarly assembled ideas embodied in the subsequent books of Dostoievsky one has to consult Dostoievsky the thinker. But even without his philosophical guidance one is by no means lost in the labyrinth so skilfully constructed by him. The atmosphere is full of enthralling mysteries; the human faces are immersed in Rembrandtesque twilight; their gaze, intense and feverish, alerts and alarms the mind, but no one able to follow the author along his tortuous path will call a halt to this fascinating and unique experience until his guide himself releases him into the habitual surroundings. And then one is overcome by the feeling of having been awakened from a nightmare, or rather of having returned home from an exceedingly strange exotic country.

Does the world of Dostoievsky really resemble the Russian Empire in the second half of the 19th century? In other words, can the works of Dostoievsky containing, as it were, a serialized nightmare at long last be read as a collection of 'historical novels'? To deal properly with this question, we have to remember that Dostoievsky's artistic ambition included from the outset the aim of portraying and thus saving his age by reflecting its image in the shining mirror of art. But we have also to remember that the essence of his and of any age was, in his conception, not some solidified sediment of the past easily discernible in it, but its budding and almost imperceptibly stirring elements, still to be discovered in the dark recesses of everyday life and brought into the limelight of art. For good or ill, all the main characters of Dostoievsky are so many pointers to the time to come. They would have been unavoidably condemned to allegorical existence symbolising abstract philosophemes were they not, thanks to their creator's realistic instinct, surrounded on all sides by a host of people representing nothing except their own individual biographies. It is the plausibly looking interaction between the two classes of actors employed by Dostoievsky which accounts for the overall impression that his world is modelled on actual unprocessed historical reality.

Among Dostoievsky's 'second class' characters, if one is allowed so to describe them, stands out the crowd of busybodies, go-betweens and gossipers designed by the author for the purpose of tightening the network of his plots and of making coincidence look plausible. They are all great talkers, and their surnames are often rooted etymologically in the realm of ornithology (e.g. Lebedev in *The Idiot* derives from *lebed*, Swan): they are flying above the scene, as it were, showing it in a bird's-eye view. Frequently exposing themselves to ridicule, they impart to the respective narrative a strain of humour, irony, and satirical wisdom. The father of Sonya (in *Crime and Punishment*) as well as Karamazov senior betray their kinship with this clan. But most striking is the fact that their language as much as the cadences of their voices are almost identical with those of Dostoievsky's respective chroniclers, and even more

71

than that, are reminiscent of the author's personal style in his non-artistic prose (e.g. in *A Writer's Diary*). This indicates that in meeting the requirements of realistic art Dostoievsky was not loth deliberately to mix tragedy with comedy and, disguised as a jester, introduced his peculiar tone of mockery into the chorus of his progeny.

A chapter apart are the women and children in Dostoievsky's art.

As far as the lowest age group is concerned, it is obvious that in a world irresistibly attracted by things to come, the youngest of the young must enjoy a privileged status. And indeed, with the progress of Dostoievsky's work in his last period, children move towards the centre of events and are in the end distinguished by an apotheosis (in the Epilogue to *The Brothers Karamazov*). There were, of course, additional reasons for Dostoievsky's childhood cult, such as the child's innocence and purity, its defencelessness, and its instinctive appeal to compassion. A superlative master in depicting the woes of the world and unredeemed suffering above all, Dostoievsky's imagination was predisposed to concentrate on the 'angelic faces' of the very young. With all that, the decisive moment remained the precedence accorded by him in this case, too, to the potentialities of any historical situation in flux. Throughout his work children represent personified promises for the future.

A theme in itself, and a rather complicated one, is the manner in which Dostoievsky painted women. The great difficulties encountered by him in gaining recognition as an artist were, no doubt, partly due to his failure to add a single masterpiece to the rich collection of female portraits created in Russia since Pushkin and Lermontov up to Turgenev and Tolstoy. Unlike the young men in the frontline of Dostoievsky's characters, each with his individual message, none of the women in touch, or rather, at cross-purposes with them was thought by the artist worthy of the insignia of an 'original idea'. In Dostoievsky's world of personified ideas engaged in an apocalyptical struggle for survival and supremacy womenfolk are no more than an auxiliary service. Quite realistically excluded from the array, women both as lovers and beloved were at best restricted to the part of catalysts revealing the inner structure of the mind of men, or, as mothers, either credited or loaded with the responsibility for their sons' good or bad instincts. The strongest among Dostoievsky's female characters are selfwilled, in love with their own pride, and unforgiving (like Katerina Ivanovna in *The Brothers Karamazov*); the most attractive are self-denying, submissive or childlike (like Sonya in *Crime and Punishment*, Dasha in *The Possessed*, and Aglaya in *The Idiot*); and when a woman embodies beauty (not the idea of beauty but perfect beauty itself), as the 'Idiot's' chosen lady, the unfortunate Nastasya Filipovna, she is foredoomed to succumb to the pranks of her deranged mind and to masculine violence. As to the females of Dostoievsky's gossiper species, they appear to be not less sexless than their male counterparts and represent together with these the facetious element in the master's work.

73

However, the discrimination against women in Dostoievsky's artistic practice was by no means an outgrowth of his theoretical anti-feminism. His overall conception of contemporary life and its dynamics implied its incompatibility with happiness or even stability in human relations generally and in love in particular. How could he, then, in this world of unfulfilled love, bring a woman to life in realistic terms who would, not discarding her feminine character, personify anything less or more concrete than a longing for the love paradise irretrievably lost? In the midst of her 'original' age-fellows of the other sex, of whom many were celibatarians by inclination, she was bound to look forsaken, thrown back on herself, and quite unpredictable. All in all, Dostoievsky's women represent nature betrayed and abandoned by man and thus exposed to the ravages of blind forces culminating in human life in sub-human quasi-entomological voluptuousness immortalized as a family trait of the Karamazovs.

It appears significant in this context that Dostoievsky paid only fleeting attention to the social structure of the environment in which he let his plots take their impetuous course. Whether it is St. Petersburg, the imperial capital, or some provincial town, everywhere the social distinctions appear immaterial. The protagonists of the dramatic events move and pursue their various ideas in a mixed society whose inherited hierarchical order seems disrupted to such an extent that the last may here easily become the first and vice versa. The whole atmosphere is permeated by the forebodings of a terrible social catastrophe, and so, inadvertently and against his own innermost intentions, Dostoievsky made perceptible the rumblings of the Russian Revolution nearly half a century before the event.

Russian critics of Dostoievsky sometimes blamed him for the dullness of his prose and asserted that his dialogues, the backbone of his narrative, suffered from the lack of differentiation between the individual modes of speech of the participants, so that the impression arose as if one endless monologue, in the author's own voice and tone, was running throughout the whole text. Anyone approaching Dostoievsky without prejudice, and especially the reader of his literary prose in the original Russian, must shrug his shoulders at such crude misstatements and be driven to the conclusion that bias let loose is apt to produce deafness not less than blindness. With all that, it would be wrong not to look for some peculiarity in Dostoievsky's writing itself which might have given cause to perceive monotony where there is such an abundance of variation in tone, diction, and rhythm of speech. How, indeed, was it possible to mishear, for instance, all the difference between the inimitable staccato of a Kirillov and the jumps and jerks in the verbiage of his co-'Possessed' Verkhovensky junior? It seems that the misreading and mishearing is due in the main to the author's inclination to let the modulations and the cadences of his personal inner voice automatically infiltrate into the language of his performers, be it his 'chroniclers', his 'gossipers', or even one or the other among the protagonists of his 'company'. And this, in turn, appears to be nothing but a characteristic manifestation of Dostoievsky's singular artistic endowment.

Like all creative artists Dostoievsky, too, lived by imagination provided with raw material by experience. However, the term 'experience' in correlation with artistic activity has more than one meaning. One artist draws mainly on external experience; the other's imagination is nourished chiefly by his own inner life; only rarely can the process of artistic creation itself be singled out as the most fruitful field within the artist's domains. Yet, this is the case of Dostoievsky the artist who, in his own view, comprised the 'poet' as well as the writer of 'novels'.

Let us remember how he defined the poet's task: 'One has first of all' – he emphasized – 'to provide oneself with one or more strong impressions actually experienced by the artist's heart.' Both the experience gained in the world outside and the innermost reaction to it appeared to him equally relevant. But then 'the artist takes over', though the poet continues to co-operate with him. The specific experience of which Dostoievsky was partaking in the final stages of bringing an artistic intention to realization is compressed in this formulation. The poet in him, this source of his unaccountable inspiration, did not abandon him until the very end of the creative process and incessantly stimulated his imagination. In the process of writing he was not depicting a sequence of episodes or images kept ready made, as it were, before his mind's eye, as if his task were only to copy them by an appropriate combination of words; the wakeful nights he usually spent when he was engaged in writing were the time of his decisive and crucial artistic experience. In the course of these vigils, the imagination of the writer frequently acquired a quasi-magical potency: previously invented episodes were perceived by him as projected into space and time: vision followed vision, and individual images grew dense, became almost tangible and looked into the eyes of their creator with the gaze of hallucinations. Under the impact of this extraordinary experience of a visionary, authentically recorded by the writer himself, the line between the outer and inner world became effaced, and their confluence is indeed the distinguishing mark of Dostoievsky's art.

The realistic character of Dostoievsky's creations is thus based on the author's genuine experience as a writer. His characters do not give the impression of invented images, nor of synthetic products composed from odds and ends of human experience of the familiar type, because they come alive straight from the soul of their creator. In fact, even before Dostoievsky released them from the *Inferno* of his study into the *Purgatorio* of his written books, they were enabled to move, to speak and to act freely, only loosely controlled by the author's initial directives. And what is still more important, he identified himself in the process of creation with each one of them, both as artist and thinker, and, with the progress of their organic growth within his soul, his artistic will increasingly gave way to their intrinsic essence and truth. They all live. For Dostoievsky imparted to them all a glitter of his poetic exaltation.

It may not be amiss to add to this a few illustrations.

77

As soon as the 'Confession' of Stavrogin, the suppressed chapter from *The Possessed*, became known, a rumour was spread about that the crime described had been perpetrated by Dostoievsky himself (cf. p. 37); the main argument in support of this conjecture was the extraordinary 'realism' of the description implicitly pointing – so the argumentation went – to the actual experience of the author. It apparently did not occur to the slanderers that Dostoievsky had at his disposal an inexhaustible source of experience quite beyond the grasp of people not distinguished by the vivifying force of his imagination. Is the description of Raskolnikov's murder with all its gruesome details less realistic? (Cf. *Crime and Punishment*, Part One, VII.) Or does one not follow the dispute between Ivan Karamazov and his 'devil' as a record of a real argument? (Book XI, IX.) No doubt, all this reflects real experience of the author, yet of an author who had in him the tremendous force to identify himself with the murderer, swinging the murderous axe, and with the libertine seducing a little girl, and with a split personality, like Ivan, in conversation with his incubus, but also with saints, with women, with children, and, of course, with himself.

And yet, despite this unsurpassed artistic faculty to extend immeasurably the boundaries of his personal experience, Dostoievsky was never threatened by the danger of losing his own identity. So he remained his own self also in all vagaries of his widely ramified thought and preserved to the end in unimpaired integrity the personal union of the artist and the thinker in his unique personality.

III

The Thinker

There is no need to be ashamed of one's idealism.
A Writer's Diary, 1876, October

The recognition of Dostoievsky as an original thinker
came even later than that of his outstanding importance as an artist. In each case one of the main
obstacles to recognition was the predominance of
accepted standards of expression. While the artistic
writings of Dostoievsky appeared to disregard the
minimum requirements of the conventional novel,
his philosophical thought found expression in a
manner which, in the view of the professional
thinkers of the time, most of them professors of
philosophy, bore the mark of diffuse and irresponsible thinking. At that time, the second half of the
19th century, Kierkegaard had not yet been discovered, Nietzsche was at best counted among the
poets and, in Russia herself, Tolstoy was regarded as
a preacher rather than a thinker.

At the turn of the century, however, with the
gradual consolidation of Dostoievsky's artistic fame,
it is already possible to record the first, though still
half-hearted, attempts to do him justice also as a
thinker in his own right. Yet, those who, like V. V.
Rozanov, realized the importance of 'bringing the
intellectual treasures left by Dostoievsky into a
system' were discouraged by the fact that the thinker

himself never tried to give a coherent exposition of his general philosophical ideas. The articles of his philosophical creed, in so far as he expressed them in his own name, are widely scattered in his journalistic writings (the essays and notes published by him since 1860 in a number of periodicals, including his personal monthly *A Writer's Diary*) as well as in letters and in records of private conversation. The recasting of all the relevant fragments into one systematic whole was in itself a hard task. But the greatest impediment appeared to be the indissoluble personal union between the thinker and the artist in Dostoievsky, which made the one indistinguishable from the other.

Indeed, we already know to what an extent the artistic work of Dostoievsky is saturated with philosophical speculation, so that many of the central characters created by him represent philosophies endowed with life, breathing, moving and acting. Does this not imply that at least some of these characters, single or taken together, were the author's mouthpieces and that his thought coincided with theirs? That was actually the common assumption of the Russian and non-Russian critics engaged since the beginning of this century on the assessment of Dostoievsky's merits as a thinker. Nearly all of them adopted the device of presenting a distillation of the essence of the world views embodied in certain artistic images of Dostoievsky (be it 'the Idiot' Prince Myshkin, the saint Zosima, or the semi-'Possessed' Shatov) as an adequate substitute for the reconstruction of his own 'system' on the basis of his lifework in its entirety. In all these cases it was presumed that the characters concerned were nearest to the author's heart and consequently also of one mind with him. It is obvious that such an approach oversimplified the problem.

There can certainly be no doubt that Dostoievsky the thinker is reflected in the convictions, thoughts and utterances of his personages; but who would be able to discover in the world created by him Dostoievsky's own singular silhouette, let alone his full-size self-portrait? Though auto-biographical components are discernible in many of his characters, none of their biographies is a replica of his. Complex and seemingly inscrutable as many of them are, Dostoievsky himself was of still greater complexity and still more of an enigma even in his own perception. This applies in particular to the various stages in the evolution of his thought. Did he not declare a decade before his death that try as one may to convey to others a 'new thought', the very essence of the new 'idea' will remain undisclosed 'even if one were to fill volumes with its explanation and keep interpreting it 35 years on end'. (Cf. *The Idiot*, Part III, end of Chap. V; Dostoievsky's literary activity lasted exactly thirty-five years, and long before the end he anticipated that he would die at sixty.) To make proper use of his artistic work in the reconstruction of his philosophy one must, therefore, first of all take care to avoid the pitfall of simplification.

If the notion that Dostoievsky occupied a niche of his own in the history of human thought is well-founded, then it must also be presumed that there exists a close correlation between his original way of thinking and his artistic inspiration. Therefore, the first question to be asked in any effort to define the true significance of this correlation is whether the world created by Dostoievsky's imagination corresponds essentially, and in its whole extension, to the author's fundamental attitudes of mind, and it seems that a full appreciation of the originality of Dostoievsky's art must implicitly suggest the sought-for answer.

We may remember that already, at the beginning of his creative life, Dostoievsky expressed his heart's desire to become 'an artist in science', and that the 'science' which he hoped to advance by artistic means was no other than a consistent moral philosophy based on a comprehensive philosophy of history. Inspired by this aim he succeeded in enriching literary art with a new synthesis of concrete imagery and abstract thought. Would it then not be right to see in this characteristic feature of his art the most promising starting point for an objective reconstruction of his theoretical world view, and to presume that its evolution was running parallel to the intensification of the productivity of his imagination? There is good reason to suppose that in the process of his evolution as a thinker Dostoievsky, instead of imparting his innermost thoughts only to a selected group of characters, brought them all into an intimate and meaningful relationship with certain aspects of his 'system' as a whole. It would at all events be rash to brush aside such a conjecture merely because Dostoievsky's characters seem to represent quite frequently irreconcilable points of view in strictly logical contradiction one to another. The answer to the question how could one and the same thinker be represented, for instance, by all the brothers Karamazov, including even Smerdyakov, might possibly be found in the assumption that it was far from Dostoievsky's mind to entrust the essence of his 'new thought' to any one of them in particular, not even to Ivan or Alyosha, but that nevertheless he needed them all to make explicit the various turns and twists of his own dialectical thinking.

In this context it may be useful once more to cite the analogy with Plato. How does one know who among the persons appearing in his Dialogues spoke for their author and to whom he assigned the part of the devil's advocate? Is Socrates, his spiritual father, and Socrates, the issue of his own mind and imagination, always one and the same person? And is Plato himself always one with Socrates or perhaps sometimes with the others – with Gorgias, Protagoras, or Parmenides? Still all these difficulties and doubts notwithstanding, no one questions the identity of Plato's philosophy in the whole process of its evolution. Could it not be that the relation of Dostoievsky's thinking to his artistic work is similar to that of Plato to his Dialogues? Surely, a symphonic dialectic reigns supreme in the world of his imagination. Is it then not appropriate to compare him with the conductor of an orchestra, who, not playing any particular instrument himself, turns his back to the audience and, swinging his magic baton, extracts from each instrument its singular individual contribution? But even such a comparison is not exact enough. For in relation to the 'orchestra' conjured up by his imaginative thought Dostoievsky is simultaneously conductor and composer of the work performed. His personal thought and way of thinking could, therefore, be discovered only in the composition as a whole projected through the composer's individual style of orchestration. This indeed is the general methodological conception underlying the following analysis.

The preliminary question as to whether Dostoievsky was sufficiently qualified to build his artistic work on philosophical foundations does not present any difficulty. We know that already at a very early age he was fascinated by the intimate relationship connecting poetry with philosophy and religion. Later he assiduously studied the philosophical classics and became particularly impressed by the exponents of German Idealism, above all by Hegel's system; when still an exile in Siberia, he even planned to translate some of Hegel's works into Russian. As to Plato, his complete works were in the last period of Dostoievsky's life constantly by his side in his private library. Parallel with his philosophical studies which as a matter of course included philosophy of history Dostoievsky pursued the study of history proper in all languages at his command. His first biographer, N. N. Strakhov, himself a philosophical scholar of repute, records that Dostoievsky was always attracted by 'questions concerning the essence of things and the limits of knowledge', and that it caused him 'amusement' whenever it was pointed out to him how

much his general ideas resembled 'various philosophical views known from the history of philosophy';
'it transpired' – relates the biographer in conclusion
– 'that it was difficult to invent something new, and
Dostoievsky jokingly reassured himself by the fact
that in his thoughts he coincided with one or the
other great thinker.'

The salient point in this account, of course, is not
the insinuation that as a thinker Dostoievsky was
prompted by a naïve ambition to 'invent' something
entirely novel, but, on the contrary, that he was
rather anxious to ascertain to what an extent his
intellectual intuition was in consonance with the
recorded history of human thought. In view of his
intimate acquaintance with this aspect of universal
history, there can be no doubt that his vast learning
was a potent factor in the gradual crystallization of
his personal philosophical creed. But is it possible
to single out the fountain-head of a specific philosophical tradition which might decisively have informed
Dostoievsky's thought enabling it also to assume
control over his art?

The prominent place accorded in his art to 'ideas'
as real entities is a clear indication that Dostoievsky
was under the spell of Plato's metaphysic and used
his theory of ideas as a safe springboard for his own
speculation. This is borne out by a close examination
of the use Dostoievsky made in all his writings, artistic as well as non-artistic, of the very term 'idea' (in
Russian *eedeya*). True, here and there he deviates from
his personal usage and implies the more common
connotations in the sense of ideal, design, principle

or abstract thought in general; but whenever his aim is to focus attention on the real essence, be it of an individual human being or of a whole nation or of a spiritual tradition, he invariably denotes it by the term 'idea' in its metaphysical, its Platonic meaning. It was, therefore, quite natural that referring to his own specific view of life he defined it as 'idealism', and it was this 'idealism' which in the domain of art provided the philosophical basis for his 'realism in a higher sense'.

Faced with the positivistic and materialistic trends which were then holding sway in Russia, and not there only, over the minds of the younger generation, Dostoievsky never tired to stress that 'in essence Idealism is exactly as realistic as Realism and can in no circumstances disappear from the world'; 'the idealist and the realist' – he explained – 'have one and the same object: Man, and they only differ as to the forms of perception of this object' (*A Writer's Diary*, 1876, July–August, Chap. 2, II). Similar statements abound in Dostoievsky's non-artistic writings of the 1870s and culminate in the address on Pushkin of 1880. However, the rehabilitation of the idealistic philosophy, including its ancient metaphysical ante-cedents, was initiated by Dostoievsky much earlier; in fact – since the world created by his art began to emerge as a new autonomous reality existing, as it were, in accordance with laws as yet undiscovered by natural science. Not questioning the validity of the general principles constituting the natural order of things, such, for instance, as the nexus between cause and effect, Dostoievsky succeeded through the medium of fiction to convey an awareness of most real links between man and man, between man and his 'idea' as well as between the 'ideas' themselves which were beyond the grasp and outside the jurisdiction of common science. Thus the artist undermined the despotic rule of the accepted 'ironcast notions', to use his phrase, and opened up a vista to a philosophy which was so much in contrast with the predominant 'scientifism' in all its varieties and so much nearer to the classical tradition of Idealism, on the one hand, and to the Christian tradition, on the other.

To Dostoievsky the point of intersection of both traditions was the concept of the 'immortality of the human soul', an 'idea' which in the end he came to identify with his own self. 'The idea of immortality' – he wrote in 1876 – 'is life itself, living life, its final formula and the source of truth and of wholesome consciousness for mankind.' Whatever else this affirmation may signify, it is clearly a profession of faith which contains the 'final formula' of Dostoievsky's personal existence, the sum total of his singular experience as artist and thinker. A close scrutiny of the context in which the quoted sentence appears and of other correlated statements dating from the same period makes it clear that in his relentless quest for a pivotal point in his own thinking he at long last discovered it in his 'unshakeable conviction' that 'immortality is beyond doubt real'. (Cf. *Diary*, 1876, October, Chap. 1, IV: December, Chap. 1, III, and letter to N. A. Ozmidov of February 1878.)

Having discovered his personal 'idea', the soul of his soul, as it were, in the awareness of the indestructible nature of his individual 'psyche', Dostoievsky thus vindicated the seemingly supernatural character of the world brought forth by his imagination; though different from the physical world comprising nothing but ephemeral phenomena in space and time, it could nevertheless claim to represent reality not less real than the human soul. In his enthusiastic self-identification with the 'idea of immortality' he contemplated the reaffirmation of his innermost 'conviction' in a logically cogent exposition, apparently intending to make use of some of Kant's arguments and to apply the 'transcendental method' of deduction. In contradistinction to Kant, however, to whom the 'transcendental ideas' God, Freedom, and Immortality were of equal significance, Dostoievsky singled out the last one as the real foundation of the other two; for – he argued – without the intuitive perception of the real existence of the immortal soul, of an entity which by definition and immediate experience was not material, no one could believe in the existence of God and no one would ever care for man's real freedom. In this respect Dostoievsky was in line with Plato and metaphysical realism in general rather than with Kant and his critical idealism.

To Dostoievsky, not less than to Plato, the 'idea' was the real thing in the midst of shadows; accordingly, he drew a sharp line between 'ideas' and general concepts, the products of generalization. (Cf. *Diary*, 1876, October, Chap. 1, II.) To him the 'idea' was as real as the concrete individual soul, since the essential uniqueness and indivisible singleness of every soul in its endless manifestations could, in his view, find no expression more adequate and concentrated than that which is attainable through the medium of the consciously or unconsciously active idea. 'There are ideas' – he explained in the essay on 'Philosophy of the Milieu' – 'which remain unexpressed, unconscious, and are only strongly felt; there are many such ideas fused together, as it were, with the soul of man. They also exist in a whole people as well as in mankind taken as a whole. So long as these ideas are unconsciously embedded in the life of the people and are merely strongly and properly felt, only so long can the people live a powerful living life. All the energy of its life is but a reflex of its strivings to make those hidden ideas clear to itself' (*Diary*, 1873, No. 2). In these few lines we have before us a concise outline of Dostoievsky's general theory of ideas, and they also indicate that he saw in his idealism a reliable instrument to unravel the mysteries of individual and historical life, and above all a clue to the true meaning of universal history.

To forestall inevitable assaults on his idealistic view of life, incompatible in its very essence with the philosophical climate of the age, Dostoievsky tried to buttress his general position by a variety of pointed aphorisms, such as: 'It is possible to know a great deal unconsciously'; 'Ideas are infectious'; 'Ideas live and spread in accordance with laws which it is too difficult for us to grasp', or, to cite yet another example, 'It can hardly be assumed that science already possesses enough knowledge of human nature that it should be able infallibly to set forth new laws of the body social' (*Diary*, 1876, December, Chap. 1, III and March, Chap. 1, IV; 1873, No. 2). These aphoristic utterances reveal that, in line with the Platonic tradition, Dostoievsky unhesitatingly accepted the existence of a realm of ideas with its own 'laws', independent of the world of common experience and yet firmly implanted in it, coexisting with it like soul and body. Any variety of idealism which divided the world into two halves, an ideal and a real one, placing the first somewhere 'beyond the stars', was rejected by Dostoievsky as 'transmundane romanticism' doomed to degenerate in our earthly life into an irresponsible 'cynicism' (*Diary*, 1876, July-August, Chap. 2).

But could an account be given also of the inner structure of Dostoievsky's realm of ideas and the direction in which he visualized its co-ordination with the physical Cosmos?

It seems that the answer to both questions may be found in Dostoievsky's instinctive Panpsychism which, intertwined with his not less spontaneous Panpersonalism, permeated his whole lifework. According to his primordial intuition, everything existing and capable of manifesting an individual character was, by this token alone, an animated entity. The paradigm was to him the human body as the dwelling place of an imperishable soul whose uniqueness was symbolized by the individual character of every human face and whose link with the world of eternity was determined by the idea engraved in it. Yet, a 'psyche' of their own could also be imputed, according to Dostoievsky, to collective entities: to peoples, to cities, and institutions, if only they revealed in the course of historical time a distinct individual character finding expression in a specific clear-cut 'idea'. In this respect Dostoievsky's thinking was undoubtedly influenced by the exponents of German Idealism of the post-Kantian period. Not only by Hegel but also by Fichte and Schelling, though they themselves would hardly ever have accepted the hyper-realistic interpretation of their metaphysics propounded by their bold follower in Russia.

Not afraid of being denounced by scientifically minded contemporaries for his indulgence in 'mystical' speculation, Dostoievsky extended to the whole sphere of historical life the application of the same pattern which, in conformity with his general theory of ideas, typified the relationship between body, soul, and idea in the life of a single human being. Precisely – he thought – as an original idea of an individual was the expression of the uniqueness of his soul, while this, in turn, was the principle of the organic unity of the living body animated by it, so every people with an historical mission, asserting its own 'idea', was endowed with an undying soul as well as with a body – i.e. its preordained homeland. Thus, speaking about the different characters of Moscow and St. Petersburg, he emphasized that nonetheless 'the soul was the same in both cities as also in all the rest of Russia, for everywhere, at every place in the whole of Russia was present Russia as a whole'. The analogy with soul and body of an individual is complete (*Diary*, 1876, May, Chap. 1, II). But it is more than an analogy, let alone a patriotic metaphor. In the same vein Dostoievsky referred to 'Italy' as the physical substratum of the 'idea' of a united human race kept alive on Italian soil since antiquity; to 'Germany' with her own 'idea' of nonconformism; to 'Europe' as a Continent faithful to the vision of a universal Christian civilization, of that 'idea' to which he himself laid claim in the name of Russia's immortal soul; and finally – to the whole Earth, the habitat of mankind whose common ideas were still immersed in the slumbering psyche of our unique planet (Cf. *Diary*, 1877, January, Chap. 1, I and Chap. 3, I: 1876, June, Chap. 2, IV; 1877, April, Chap. 2, III). In short, Dostoievsky based his philosophy of history on the assumption that the ideas whose evolution, interplay, and collision made human history meaningful were linked by the souls of the historical nations with the respective physical conditions of their earthly life. This was, incidentally, the source of Dostoievsky's vivid interest in current international affairs in which, in his view, the nations were always involved with body, soul, and idea.

Dostoievsky's historical Panpsychism implied that his ideal world was not divorced from the real world in space and time, but on the contrary fitted into the same universe which is the object of natural science. The inner structure of his world of ideas largely coincided therefore with the network of mutual relations which are, in the traditional and popular view, constitutive for any community of human souls. In essence, we can say, the fabric is the same, if only we do not overlook that, according to Dostoievsky's Panpersonalism, every human soul is, at least potentially, a person distinguished by its own idea which is the soul of its soul.

It was this metaphysical background of his art which prompted Dostoievsky to describe himself as a 'realist in a higher sense'. Not claiming inside knowledge of a purely spiritual world, he tried to demonstrate that a truly realistic treatment of human nature could not ignore and should not neglect its ideal dimension. In the last resort, he felt, all relations between human beings were determined by the direct contact of their souls experienced either consciously, through the medium of their respective 'ideas', or unconsciously, as in the case of love relations between man and woman. Accordingly, Dostoievsky had no inhibitions to re-examine biological phenomena, including heredity, in the light of his realistic idealism.

A detailed analysis of Dostoievsky's allusive accounts concerning the succession of generations within any one of his 'accidental families' proves beyond doubt that procreation and physical descent were to him tantamount to a process of filiation of ideas. It remains uncertain, for instance, whether Verkhovensky junior, the cynical ringleader of the 'Possessed', was his father's son or his 'nephew'; this may appear awkward indeed, if one does not remember that the 'father' himself, Verkhovensky senior, stands revealed as the personification of twin-ideas: of that abstract pseudo-idealism which carries unmitigated cynicism with it as its reverse. The offspring of this dual personality, the personification of unqualified cynicism can, therefore, be regarded as a descendant not only of his father but also – and rather more correctly – of his father's twin brother, as it were, that is of his 'uncle' (Cf. *The Possessed*, Part One, Chap. 2, VI and Part Two, Chap. 4, II). Such subtly concealed hints served Dostoievsky's purpose to infiltrate the texture of his narratives with the essence of his speculative thought.

Another more comprehensive illustration of Dostoievsky's metaphysical interpretation of heredity is contained in the matrimonial chronicle of the Karamazov family. The four sons of old Karamazov are the children of three different mothers. They are all in various degrees tinged by their father's peculiar idea which is, in essence, a passionate affirmation of life liable to explode in fits of frenzied voluptuousness almost indistinguishable from animal lust. However, every one of the four sons lives up to his own original idea in which the father's consuming thirst for life is but a component. Mitya, the eldest, is the fruit of his father's union with a 'hot-tempered, courageous, swarthy, impatient lady of remarkable physical strength'. In this union the naked idea of life for life's sake collided with another living soul, and it is on record that Fyodor Karamazov's first wife used to 'thrash' him. In consequence, the idea of his firstborn son is to force upon himself a ruthless mastery over his wild propensities; it is the idea of man's innate faculty to assert his privileged position in the physical world by taming his chaotic subhuman instincts. A Karamazov like his father, Mitya personifies the rebellion of human nature against itself in the name of a humanism which must unavoidably be chaotic at its first awakening.

Thus, the thesis represented by an older generation fatefully collides with its antithesis in the succeeding generation and expands farther towards the germination of a synthesis, i.e. towards the idea of human perfection. The two aspects of this idea, the secular and the traditional Christian, are embodied in the two younger brothers, Ivan and Alyosha. Sons of the same mother, 'the humble and meek Sophia', they are meant to supplement one another, while their mother's name stands for Russia's still subconscious unuttered 'Wisdom' slowly maturing through suffering.

There still remains the fourth brother, the horrible Smerdyakov. Almost an outsider, he nevertheless also personifies an 'original idea' rooted in the Karamazov breeding ground – that of extreme rationalism culminating in the exultation of formal logic. His existence is a by-product of his father's measureless lust for life and power. Impelled by his extravagant life-affirmation the father had found gratification in taking possession of a vagrant imbecile, with the result that the offspring of the unholy union evinces the idea that the unredeemed fortuity of individual existence must be counterbalanced by generalizing reason mercilessly nullifying the specific differences of being. In this genealogical frame Smerdyakov's moral insanity stands out as a concomitant of his perverted intellectualism which is thus exposed as a fatal fallacy threatening to bring to nought even the noblest aspirations of his half-brother Ivan.

The complex set-up of the Karamazov family enabled Dostoievsky to interlace the tangled web of his narrative with a multitude of very thin, almost imperceptible lines of thought pointing from various directions to that general genealogy of ideas which was conceived by him as the real substratum of an adequate philosophy of history and, consequently, as the basis for a realistic moral philosophy. Since the early 1860s, his goal in both these coalescing fields was the assessment of the stage reached by the human race in the gradual evolution of ideas from generation to generation, and the evaluation, on the strength of this appraisal, of the prospects for a moral regeneration of humanity. For, since his first journey abroad, in 1862, he was firmly convinced that the moral crisis in the West was not less devastating than the vacillations of mind and philosophical aberrations endemic among the Russian intelligentsia.

It may well be that the conception of a genealogical tree of ideas had developed in Dostoievsky's mind in deliberate opposition to Charles Darwin's *Origin of Species* published just three years before the Russian adept of philosophical spiritualism set foot on English soil. A full record of the indelible impact made on Dostoievsky by the technological civilization and, in particular, by its gigantic shop window, the London World Exhibition of 1862, can be found in his incisive *Notes from the Underground* In this semi-philosophical, semi-artistic inquiry Dostoievsky's intention of advancing his method of investigation into the genealogy of ideas, as a kind of antidote against the scientific approach to the delineation of man's place in nature, becomes clearly discernible. Here, moreover, we find the reason which prompted him to restrict the field of his investigation to Russia. His 'anti-hero', as the fictitious author of the *Notes* describes himself, is a 'Russian European', which means that he represents the Russian 'educated class' in its eagerness to assimilate the ripest fruits of Europe's civilization in order to judge their intrinsic value from the inside, as it were. In other words, the life story of Dostoievsky's 'anti-hero' is synchronized with that critical stage in the evolution of ideas at which Russia's partnership in the European legacy markedly gained momentum and which brought the Russian intelligentsia to the dilemma whether to join the general trends of European thought or to blaze its path into the future independently. As to Dostoievsky himself, in the light of his experience abroad, his choice was obvious. Although it would be wrong to identify the actual author of the *Notes* with his anti-hero, it remains true that both were reasoning on parallel lines. In fact, the same philosophical problems which tormented the mind of the First Person Singular of the *Notes* did not cease to harass Dostoievsky himself till the end of his life. Was human freedom still an attainable goal under the reign of natural science? If not, how can human consciousness avoid disintegration in the setting of our time? These were the essentially moral problems which occupied Dostoievsky.

Indeed – asked Dostoievsky – what would freedom mean if the scientific approach to human nature were the only one possible? Natural science recognises only phenomena in space and time interconnected by innumerable chains of causes and effects by which the individual is so tightly hemmed in that, being aware of what science stands for, he does not even dare to claim for himself the dignity of a free agent. However, continuing the line of thought pursued by Dostoievsky since his fascinating experience in the Western temples of triumphant science, the voice 'from underground' exclaims: 'Where from shall I take primordial causes to lean on? Where – the grounds? I practise thinking and, therefore, any primordial cause drags another still more primordial one immediately in its wake and so *ad infinitum*. This is the very essence of all consciousness and thinking' (*Notes*, etc. Part 1, V). Like his imaginary thinker Dostoievsky was fully aware that, apart from the endless external physical world, there existed yet another infinity, that which man might discover within his own consciousness, and that it was precisely this inner human endlessness where a solution of the crucial problem of human freedom in a world of necessity ought to be sought and could perhaps be found. If the Western world which first brought to light the significance of man's awareness of his own self (Descartes' *Cogito ergo sum*) was about to surrender its great philosophical tradition to the powers that be, to exact science and the laws of nature, then,

Dostoievsky thought, it was incumbent on the 'Russian Europeans', including himself, to pick up the broken thread and to think for themselves. With his general theory of ideas as a basis and forearmed by his intuitive knowledge of the immortality of the human soul, Dostoievsky carried out in his artistic laboratory a series of thought experiments designed with the dual purpose of disproving pseudo-philosophical approaches to the freedom problem, and of pointing to its proper place in the consciousness of the individual. Just as Dostoievsky reveals himself as an original thinker through the medium of his art, his art will appear in a clearer perspective when perceived through the medium of his spontaneous thinking.

The first great experiment in the series devised by Dostoievsky for the exploration of the ways and means at the disposal of modern man in his struggle for the survival of human freedom is recorded in the story of Raskolnikov (*Crime and Punishment*). Raskolnikov is conceived as a true son of the new age, free from the so-called religious superstitions and entirely in line with modern positivism equating reality with what empirical science knows about it. But he is also a 'Russian European' who cannot look away from his own blurred consciousness and disregard his intense longing for absolute independence. Thus an 'original idea' imposes itself on his whole being: if there is nothing in the world but pure and simple factuality – he reasons – whence could then be derived a criterion for the distinction of good and evil? This implies that a consistent follower of the positivistic philosophy is *a priori* justified in transgressing at will any norm of conduct, that he is absolutely free to deal with other human beings at his own discretion, and generally to behave as though he was the sovereign of the universe.

On the face of it, it may appear that this Individualism incarnate solves the problem of human freedom at least for one person. But even this, as Dostoievsky tries to demonstrate *ad oculos*, is not true. The price of such absolute freedom is absolute loneliness, absolute isolation, and where there is no Second Person, either in the plural or in the singular, even a godlike First Person hovering above good and evil is bound to discover in the end that it is no person at all, but a phantom among phantoms. Instead of solving the problem of freedom, positivistic individualism deprives it of meaning and precipitates the disintegration of individual consciousness. Raskolnikov's apocalyptic dream in his Siberian prison puts the seal on his philosophy: it exposes his original idea and the crime engendered by it as a symptom of the general mental disarray of the age, and is a stern warning against worse things to come. If no heed were to be taken of this and similar warnings – this is the message conveyed by Raskolnikov's nightmarish vision – the whole of mankind would be engulfed by universal infectious madness resulting in a war of all against all and of everyone against everyone else; but even then, on the very verge of total extinction, the infected ones will as never before rely on their reasoning and cling 'to their scientific deductions'. Salvation may hinge on the survival of a few pure souls 'predestined to incept a new human race and new life on a rejuvenated and purified earth' (*Crime and Punishment*, Epilogue II). As in a number of analogous thought experiments Dostoievsky applied in his argumentation the method of reducing the contested proposition *ad absurdum*, contrasting it by significant allusions to the highest goal of his own thinking.

On the last page of *Crime and Punishment* devoted to the prospects of the 'criminal's' spiritual regeneration our eye meets the reassuring words: 'Replacing dialectics there entered life, and something entirely different was bound to take shape in his consciousness'. The notion implied in this sentence that dialectical thinking divorced from real life must of necessity lead astray is one of the principles which guided Dostoievsky in all his philosophical experiments. And there was no truer and loftier manifestation of life for Dostoievsky than that which revealed itself in love. For love in which one immortal soul found immediate access to the core of another unique and immortal being, this alone was the real safeguard against the threat of absolute isolation inherent in any 'original idea' rebelling against the spiritual 'commonwealth of ideas' and groping on its own for an outlet from the maze of dialectics. It is remarkable that Dostoievsky pronounced his word of warning already in the laconic summing-up of the *Notes from Underground*. Entrusting his 'anti-hero' with the representation of all exponents of modern speculative separatism and isolationism, he wrote in their name: 'We are stillborn, and what is more, for quite a while we are being born not by living fathers, and we like it more and more. We have got the taste of it. Soon we shall contrive somehow to be born by an idea.' In fact, already then Dostoievsky saw clearly that his genealogical tree of ideas enshrined in the succession of living generations was in danger of being torn out by the roots.

His anguish as to 'the possibility of a continuation of world history' is most tellingly reflected in the image of the 'possessed' Kirillov, the would-be deicide. Like Ivan Karamazov later on, Kirillov personifies the idea of man's rivalry with the Creator of the universe. To both, God is a reality, but while Ivan rises in dialectical armour to expose the moral deficiency of God's creation, Kirillov sets out to discard God altogether as a fictitious hypostasis of man's 'fear of the pain of death', in order to clear the way for the transfiguration of humanity into a divine entity: Man should become God. As a typical 'Russian European' who, moreover, had some experience even of America, he strongly believes in the experimental method; if, he thinks, he would commit suicide for no other reason than for the sake of proving that man was capable to free himself from the deadly fear of death, the 'main freedom' would be conquered and man's power would become limitless. With his bold hyper-dialectical idea in mind, Kirillov sees himself in the mirror of his consciousness as though he already possessed the power to destroy and recreate the world, as if he were in fact identical with God on the threshold of creation, making the choice between the divine 'Let there be' and self

elimination. (Cf. *The Possessed*, I, Chap. 3, VIII.)
This whole monstrosity of God contemplating
suicide might have been invented by Dostoievsky as
a counterblast against Auguste Comte's Positivism
culminating in his 'Religion of Humanity'. Once
more a popular philosophical position was probed
by the method of *reductio ad absurdum*.

However, in its general form Kirillov's idea that
suicide was a shortcut to the solution of the freedom
problem was taken by Dostoievsky most seriously.
In three consecutive issues of his *Diary* he discussed
at length the temptation haunting the enlightened
atheist of the scientific age to assert the freedom of
his will by cutting the line of his own life (*A Writer's
Diary*, 1876, October–December). Every single case
of suicide which came to Dostoievsky's knowledge
struck his imagination, tormented his mind and
spurred his sense of guilt. For, perhaps even more
than laxity towards another creature's life, the allure-
ments of suicide appeared to him as a 'logical' consequence of the ascendancy of the world view which
rejected the validity of the spiritual and condemned
man to solitary confinement within his own self; yet,
knowing what he knew – whispered to Dostoievsky
his guilty conscience – was he not personally responsible for the fact that close to him, in his own Russia,
terrible things did not cease to happen, whereas he
merely registered and analysed them?

In any appraisal of Dostoievsky's thought it is not
irrelevant to bear in mind that he himself was the
most exacting judge of his metaphysical hypotheses.
Applying all his artistic skill in testing them by

confrontation with real life, he singled out in his imagination murder and suicide as the most revealing projections of self-centered 'pride'. But – he thought – the fatal self-adoration may overreach itself to such an extent that, to overcome his absolute isolation, the 'proud man' of the new age might even contemplate the creation by sheer willpower of another human being whose relationship to the self-appointed creator would be similar to that of man to God. Quite appropriately the account of such an experiment, recorded in the short story *The Meek One*, was inserted by Dostoievsky among his reflections on suicide, because in the case in point the meek creature, 'born', as it were, by the embodiment of an 'original idea', was foredoomed to throw away her artificial existence. (Cf. *Diary*, 1876, November.)

It may be pertinent to ask in conclusion whether Dostoievsky's metaphysical resources were sufficient to balance his sinister diagnosis of the time's diseases by a reasonable hope for recovery in the future. For that much is certain: his thinking, as his art, were inspired by the same painful anxiety not to miss the point at which the decline of Christian civilization might be brought to a halt and its downward movement reversed towards a new uplift. It seems, however, that the only remedial asset at his disposal was his reliance on the efficacy of the 'Russian idea'. This, as expounded with ardent enthusiasm by Dostoievsky in his Pushkin speech, was the genuinely Christian endeavour of the Russian people to bring about a 'universal reconciliation of ideas', i.e. the harmonization of all the great ideas which left their mark in world history, combined with the people's unconditional trust, that the Russian idea, as the very essence of the Christian faith was predestined to conquer the whole of humanity. (Cf. *Diary*, 1880, August, Chap. 1–2 II.)

Has Russia given the lie to the prophetic message of Dostoievsky's philosophy? Has the subsequent course of Russian and universal history exposed his thinking as illusory and deceptive? Dostoievsky himself might have countered these and similar sardonic questions by reiterating what he wrote in his own name nearly a hundred years ago: 'In the end the triumph belongs not to material forces, frightful and unshakeable as they may seem, not to wealth, not to the sword, not to power, but to some at first unnoticeable thought often deriving from the apparently humblest of men' (*A Writer's Diary*, 1876, December, Chap. 1, III.)

These are proud words, indeed, but they derive from one whose humbleness was as genuine as his faith.

IV

The Significance

> . . . Perhaps I am indeed a philosopher, and, who
> knows, may be I really have the intention to
> teach . . .
>
> L. N. Myshkin in *The Idiot*, I, V

The emergence of Dostoievsky above the horizon of
world literature, soon after that of Turgenev and
almost coincidentally with Tolstoy, signifies a remarkable turn in the flow of ideas which had, in the
18th century, brought Russia into the ambit of West
European thought. Before the reception by the
Western world of the 'Russian novel' as an original
form of artistic writing, Russia seemed predestined
in the sphere of creative endeavour to play the modest
part of a beneficiary of European civilization, of a
latecomer diligently striving to live up to the standards set up by the foreign masters. However, such
an approach became untenable at the turn of the 19th
century. The breaking out of Russia's literature from
its linguistic confinement, with Tolstoy and Dostoievsky as its two-pronged spearhead, revealed that
the vast colony of European civilisation in the
Nearest East was the homeland of an independent
cultural potential, though European in the external
forms of its manifestations, yet different in tendency
and content. Thus, the discovery of the basic
originality of Russia's literature, ushered in by its

twin giants, entailed a partial reversal in the broad movement of European thought: instead of advancing as heretofore in a unique sense, from West to East, it also comprised from that time onwards a current flowing in the opposite direction, from Russia towards the West.

Alongside with the typical Russian *roman* (the 'russan' as a French conoisseur nicknamed the over-size narrations of Tolstoy and Dostoievsky), there appeared in quick succession many other forms of Russian literary production on the Western scene: specimens of Russia's dramatic art, of short and long stories, of literary criticism and philosophical essays, until the steadily growing interest in the newly dis-covered literature encompassed even Russian poetry, its least accessible province. This process of assimila-tion of the Russian cultural patrimony, at long last extending to the integration of the Russian tongue itself into the family of foreign languages taught and spoken in the West, produced in its wake a strong disposition to differentiate between things Russian and, in particular, to single out from among their exponents those who stood on their own feet, in-dependently of the country of their origin. It was this deeper discernment that led in the end to the realization that Dostoievsky was important for his own sake. And this, moreover, not only because he was one of the most prominent Russian authors, a master comparable with Turgenev and Tolstoy, or, for that matter, with Balzac and Dickens, but first and foremost because his name signified a powerful challenge reaching out far beyond the boundaries of self-contained art; because his singular message was intrinsically a vehement call directed to the whole of humanity in the cause of humanity's highest aspirations.

The gradual rise of Dostoievsky towards the summit of human greatness; his elevation to the dignity of a religious teacher, as it were, is in itself a striking illustration of the general change in the spiritual relations between the Western world and Russia, which began to gain momentum from the first decade of the 20th century. The 'Russian novel' had opened the floodgates for the influx not only of Russian artistic and intellectual values; thanks to their subsequent assimilation by the West, it had also prepared the ground for a better understanding of the Russian character and of the specific Russian sensibility. From understanding sprang forth an inclination to emulate the Russian attitude of mind. To cite one instance only, the so-called Dostoievsky cult – a characteristic feature of English literary life after the publication of *The Brothers Karamazov* in 1912 – would scarcely have had a chance of developing had not the image of Dostoievsky himself under the impact of his work acquired among his admirers the semblance of an icon to be worshipped *à la russe*. This is all the more noteworthy when we take into account that in Dostoievsky's own homeland his significance was at that time still a controversial issue and even his stature as artist not sufficiently appreciated.

True, in the course of the thirty-three years that passed from Dostoievsky's death to the outbreak of the First World War (1881–1914) the challenging force of his 'cruel talent', in the phrase of one of the most influential Russian critics of the period, N. K. Mikhaylovsky, remained a catalytic factor within the literary, philosophical and political trends among the Russian intelligentsia. But his prophetic image which had begun to take shape towards the end of the 1870s and fired the imagination of the multitude during the Pushkin celebrations in Moscow in 1880 melted away like a phantom a few years after his death. There were weighty reasons for the anticlimax. The assassination of Tsar Alexander II in March 1881 inaugurated a ruthless political reaction which lasted throughout the reign of his successor, Alexander III (1881–94); the new Tsar drew his inspiration from Russia's 'Grand Inquisitor', Pobedonoszev, who had maintained an intimate friendship with Dostoievsky at the close of his life. Whatever else his name might have meant to the great majority of Russia's enlightened classes, his posthumous ill-fame as a 'reactionary' blinded them to the depth of his thought and even to the superb mastery of his art.

A notable exception was the philosopher and poet Vladimir Solovyov (1853–1900), allegedly the prototype of Dostoievsky's Ivan Karamazov, whose influence on Russian thoughts and letters began, however, to make itself felt only at the turn of the century. Until then, his affirmation of Dostoievsky's providential importance for the future of Christendom met with but little response. It is even doubtful whether the rising appreciation of Solovyov's philosophy stimulated the rediscovery of Dostoievsky about the middle of the 1890s or, whether on the contrary, Solovyov himself found an easier access to the heart and mind of the younger generation thanks to the new turn of the tide in favour of Dostoievsky which was due to the cumulative effect of his writings in a spontaneously expanding circle of perceptive readers. At all events, on the threshold of the 20th century, Dostoievsky and Solovyov came to the fore linked together, as though they were closely allied, exhorting Russia's intelligentsia almost with one voice to self-examination. Dostoievsky's belief that 'ideas are infectious', that they 'float above the ground' and that 'there is a penetrating force in them' proved apposite to his own case.

And yet, the association of the two ideas 'Solovyov' and 'Dostoievsky' in the mind of the Russian *élite* brought about consequences partly detrimental to a clear understanding of Dostoievsky's message. Solovyov was a mystic and a visionary in the classical sense. His philosophical speculation not less than his poetry and practical work was inspired by an experience of quite an extraordinary character. His enthusiastic activity for the sake of Christian unity, his ardent faith in the Messianic mission of Russia, his uncompromising fight for the rights of the underprivileged – all this emanated in his own feeling from a single source, the divine presence within him. In stark contrast to such mystically sustained impregnability of faith and trust in his destiny, Dostoievsky was never able to free himself entirely from the fetters of doubt and self-distrust: in his sight every human being, including his own self, revealed them-

selves as unfathomable mysteries, and even the Elder
Zosima, Dostoievsky's image of Christian perfection,
was made to share the Kantian view, according to
Alyosha Karamazov's notes, that 'it is impossible to
grasp the essence of things in earthly life'. Still, the
fact that Solovyov identified himself with Dostoievsky's legacy and appeared to be the legitimate
executor of his will implicitly suggested that both
apostles of Russian Messianism could best be defined
as adepts of Christian mysticism. Far as it was from
Dostoievsky's mind to argue on the strength of
mystical experience, be it his own or that of others,
henceforth many attempts at assessing the significance of his thought and art were vitiated, first in
Russia and then in the West, by the preconceived
notion that his was the art and thought of a 'mystic',

In Russia it was mainly Merezhkovsky (1865–1941)
who laid particular stress on the mystical character
of Dostoievsky's world perspective. From the fact
that to Dostoievsky man was fundamentally a
'mystery', Merezhkovsky inferred that such a conception must have originated from a supernatural,
mystical source. For the same reason, however,
Kant, the father of German classical Idealism, who
demonstrated the endlessness of the task implied in
human cognition of any individual phenomenon,
might have been characterized as an adept of irra-
tionalistic mysticism. Yet the shibboleth for the
distinction between idealism and mysticism is just
the realization that absolute knowledge, though a
constant aim and propelling factor within the
human mind, by definition transcends the limits of

its legitimate sphere of operation. Virtually, Dostoievsky's Idealism placed him nearer to the rationalistic bias of Tolstoy than to the celestial mysticism of Solovyov. Nevertheless, for a lengthy and highly critical period in the evolution of Russian thought, Merezhkovsky's pronouncements remained practically unchallenged and provided the philosophical basis for his antithetical juxtaposition *Tolstoy and Dostoievsky* (the title of Merezhkovsky's work published in 1901–2) which actually pointed to the incompatibility of Tolstoy's rationalism with Dostoievsky's mysticism.

One of the results of this trenchant approach was the bifurcation of the Russian literary tradition deriving from Pushkin into two contending trends, a Tolstoyan and a Dostoievskyan. The theme 'Tolstoy versus Dostoievsky' (or vice versa) gained the impressiveness of a *leitmotiv* which brought into the subsequent history of Russian letters an element of drama, keeping alive ever since a sense of inner tension among writers and readers alike. Whereas the novelists, storytellers, and dramatists, with Gorky and his school in the forefront, who were content with the conventional notion of reality, looked up to Tolstoy as to the unsurpassed master of realistic art, the partisans of Russian Symbolism (the new school emerging in the 1890s under French influence), to whom the seemingly real everyday life was but an allusion to metaphysical realities behind it, emphatically stressed the greater importance of Dostoievsky as the standard bearer of a new age in art and life. It is certainly no accident that the founders of the new school simultaneously excelled as prose writers and poets. This applies to some extent to Merezhkovsky himself, the most influential spokesman of the new movement, but particularly to his wife, Zinaida Gippius, to Vyacheslav Ivanov, and even more so to Fyodor Sologub, the pre-eminent and prolific poet whose novel *The Little Demon* (1907) is a masterpiece informed throughout by the Dostoievskyan climate. The frequency of cases of such a personal union between novelist and poet among the Russian symbolists of the older and younger generation suggests that their attraction towards Dostoievsky, in preference to Tolstoy, reflected the unusual complexity of their own creative personalities predisposed to come down on the side of the odd and intricate rather than on that of the serene and plausible. Indeed, they were all yearning for spiritual redemption and shared in the feeling that neither they themselves nor the destiny of the new age could ever find fulfilment other than through the transformation of the surrounding 'coarse life' into a shining poetical myth holding out the promise of a final miraculous transfiguration of being. It was alleged that all this originated from affinity with Dostoievsky, and so he himself was saddled with a responsibility liable to obscure the original meaning of his message.

Although Tolstoy on the very eve of his departure, in 1910, reaffirmed his indebtedness to the author of *The Possessed* as a moralist, and Gorky, too, though utterly rejecting the 'ideas' of Dostoievsky, felt impelled on many occasions to extol him as an artist whose genius, as he once said, 'was comparable only with that of Shakespeare', the co-existence of the two antagonistic tendencies in Russian literature survived the revolution of 1917 and is discernible in the literary life of the Soviet Union (as well as of the *emigrés* abroad) even today. This is all the more remarkable in view of the fact that the Soviet government, taking its bearings chiefly from Gorky, deliberately waged an 'ideological war' against Dostoievsky. In the 1920s many of his writings were treated as if they were placed on a Soviet 'index of prohibited books', while the publication of Tolstoy's complete works, in ninety volumes, proceeded undisturbed under governmental auspices. Nothing was more encouraging to a Soviet author than a critical assessment pointing to the Tolstoyan element in his work, and nothing was more damaging than the tracing of an author's origins to the Dostoievskyan school. The scholarly exploration of Dostoievsky's life and the analysis of his artistic skill were alone to remain immune from interdiction. In so far, however, as his thinking and the deeper meaning of his legacy were concerned, he had to be shown up as a 'reactionary', an 'anarchist' and above all as an inveterate 'mystic' who had barefacedly indulged in exposing himself as a traitor to the socialist ideals of his youth. From the point of view of the predominant Marxian philosophy the last count of the indictment, addiction to mysticism, was the severest of the proferred accusations, because mysticism was by definition both reactionary and at the root of any extreme individualism anarchically opposing the authority of the state and the established social order.

True, Tolstoy also refused to recognize the supreme authority of law and order maintained by violence, but, in contrast to Dostoievsky, he appealed to reason and not to some contemptible source of revelation. Strange as it may seem, the deprecation of Dostoievsky's message under Communist rule was based on a misconception taken over by Soviet censorship and criticism on trust from the much abused 'decadents', i.e. from Merezhkovsky and his followers. All the same, the damage done by the identification of Dostoievsky's 'realism in a higher sense' with Merezhkovsky's doctrine of salvation, with Vyacheslav Ivanov's 'mystical anarchism', or with Sologub's 'Mythology' is still not repaired and continues to confound the issue.

On the other hand, the almost unimpeded freedom of research into the source material relating to Dostoievsky's biography and craftsmanship released a broad stream of valuable publications, including the carefully edited Correspondence (1928, 1934, 1959), which provide the historian of Russian literature aspiring to unprejudiced objectivity, where-ever he may be, with a solid body of reliable information. Evidently, in the innately lopsided literature wheat and straw must be kept strictly apart, and its references to the evolution, or rather 'degeneration', of Dostoievsky as a thinker unfortunately nearly always fall into the second category. But taken as a whole, the steady expansion of this literature indirectly bears witness that the realization of Dostoievsky's exceptional significance grew in intensity throughout the Soviet Union in the teeth of official policy. The fight is not over yet. Nevertheless, it seems particularly fitting on this occasion to rhyme 'word' and 'sword' in the proverbial sense. The future historian may find that just as Dostoievsky proved right in his fearful anticipation of the Revolution to come, the revolutionary oligarchy did not err in the apprehension that there was in Dostoievsky a threat to any authoritarian establishment.

In the West, the Soviet campaign against the disruptive character of Dostoievsky's world perception helped rather than hampered the recognition of his significance as a philosopher. In contrast to the literature in Soviet Russia which had no other choice but to concentrate on the minutia of the origins, composition and interdependence of Dostoievsky's works, the Dostoievsky scholars in the West turned their attention mostly to comment and interpretation. Creative artists and thinkers conferred on him, against negligible opposition, the title of master and teacher. The modern 'philosophical novel' may be claimed as his progeny. But it is not easy any longer to single out with precision his specific influence on the literature and thought of the 20th century. In this respect, Existentialism presents an outstanding exception, in so far as its exponents themselves invoked the name of Dostoievsky as that of one of their immediate predecessors. Speaking in a general way, it is not too much to say that since Russian literature has been adopted as an integral part of Western humanistic education, Dostoievsky is being regarded, even more than Tolstoy, as the embodiment of its original tradition. At all events, it seems undeniable that the presence of a Dostoievskyan strain (to some, the 'Dostoievskyan virus') in the atmosphere of the modern world is a characteristic symptom of the age. And as to the narrower confines of literary art, the student of world literature might be justified in drawing a line between its pre-Dostoievsky and post-Dostoievsky periods, for it could be said with good reason that the modern conception of the human condition has been developing in the dim light, or more precisely, in the Rembrandtesque twilight, projected *ex oriente*, from the Nearest East, and radiated by its seer Dostoievsky.

His fame as 'seer' was acquired by Dostoievsky both in Russia and in the West in the main owing to his so-called 'psychological discoveries'. His artistic presentation of the individual appeared to preclude further treatment of concrete human beings *more geometrico*, as though they were mere combinations of mathematically defined frozen features. Long before Bergson, Dostoievsky discovered that the 'Law of contradiction' does not apply to 'lively life'. The evolution of empirical research into man's inner life towards a discipline deliberately ignoring its problematical substratum, i.e. towards a 'psychology without psyche', impelled the seekers after the soul to look for its recovery outside the scientific field, first of all in the domain of articulate art. Here they came across Dostoievsky meeting them half-way with a vigorously outstretched hand. His art was fashioned to serve as an instrument of understanding. From him one learned, what one might have instinctively felt already, that every single human being is a singular mystery, a dynamic entity, though rooted in its environment and age, yet endowed with the faculty to rise above the human condition and to embrace eternity. In a sense, this was not the revelation of a new truth but the resuscitation of a very old and perennial one. Yet, at a juncture when man seemed resolved to discard his soul, Dostoievsky made it visible to the eye that behind the flattened two-dimensional image of the individual human being there was a third dimension pointing vertically to the highest heights of existence as well as to its deepest depths. It is, therefore, natural that modern analytical psychology bent on the 'scientific' exploration of the mind's 'depths' fully accepts the relevance of Dostoievsky's discoveries.

However, no appreciation of Dostoievsky's significance would be complete without special reference to the moral implications of the discoveries he made as artist and thinker. Once more – he was no 'mystic'. He firmly believed that the moral principles guiding him were basically rational. By emphasizing the mysterious aspect of human existence he tried to place all relations between individuals, and consequently between the individual and the community, on unchallengeable moral ground. If the other is no less of a 'mystery' to me than I am to myself, then my responsibility in judging the other is at least as great as when I face my own conscience looking for extenuating circumstances. As no one who is aware of the limits of his self-knowledge would condemn himself irrevocably, so the respect for the endless potentialities hidden in the existence of others would compel one to revise again and again one's conception of their essence. Moreover, the real ground of remaining an enigma unto oneself is the fact that the Ego perceives itself as a unique entity indeterminable by general abstract concepts; so is any other human being never a cipher, never an example of a generally defined group and not an agglomerate of abstract notions, but an intensely concrete person with a unique face, a unique soul and a unique destiny.

Thus, Dostoievsky's Panpersonalism becomes explicit. As a practical programme it has the advantage that, in spite of its utopian overtones, it can be put into operation by everyone here and now. Its appeal is directed to the conscience of the individual, in which it may touch responding chords or cause embarrassment and irritation. It was not by chance that decade after decade Dostoievsky had to make his way against tempestuous headwinds in his homeland. Still, the significant fact is that he survived all adversities of recent history, inside and outside his native country, and that his message is as full of meaning today as it was in his lifetime.

BIOGRAPHICAL DATES

1821. Born in Moscow on 30 October.

1833–7. At boarding schools in Moscow.

1837. Mother's death; Pushkin killed in a duel; Fyodor moves with elder brother, Mikhail, to St. Petersburg.

1838. Enters Engineering College.

1839. Father assassinated by mutinous serfs.

1841. Receives commission.

1843. Transferred to the Corps of Military Engineers.

1844. Relinquishes commission and takes up writing as a profession.

1846. Publication of *Poor People* and *The Double*.

1847–9. Publication of *The Landlady, Netochka Nezvanova* and *White Nights*; becomes involved in anti-governmental activities.

1849. Arrest, trial, and death sentence, commuted to four years' penal servitude and subsequent service in the ranks in Siberia.

1850–4. Penal servitude in Omsk.

1854–9. Military service in Semipalatinsk.

1855. Nicholas I succeeded by Alexander II.

1856. Dostoievsky restored to officer's rank.

1857. Marries the widowed Maria Isayeva.

1859. Retires from the army and returns to St. Petersburg, publishes *My Uncle's Dream* and *The Village of Stepanchikovo*.

1861–5. Co-editing, with his brother Mikhail, the monthlies *Vremya* ('Time') and *Epokha* ('Epoch') where *Notes from the House of the Dead, Insulted and Injured, Winter Notes on Summer Impressions*, and *Notes from the Underground* appear.

1862. First journey abroad (Germany, France, England).

1864. Death of his wife Maria and of his brother Mikhail.

1866. *Crime and Punishment*; *The Gambler*.

1867. Marries Anna Snitkina.

1867–71. Life abroad (Dresden, Geneva, Florence).

1868. *The Idiot*.

1870. *The Eternal Husband*.

1872. *The Possessed* (or *The Devils*).

1873–80. *A Writer's Diary*, comprising *The Meek One* (1876) and *The Dream of a Ridiculous Man* (1877).

1875. *The Raw Youth*.

1879–80. *The Brothers Karamazov*.

1880. *Pushkin Speech*.

1881. Dostoievsky dies in St. Petersburg on 28 January.

BIBLIOGRAPHY

Standard editions of Dostoievsky's works:

The first edition of Dostoievsky's complete works in 12 volumes, which included three volumes of *A Writer's Diary*, appeared in St. Petersburg in 1894–5 (*Polnoye Sobraniye Sochineniy*, with an introduction by V. V. Rozanov). Another edition, in 21 volumes, followed in 1911, also in St. Petersburg. After the revolution, the 'Gosizdat' (State Publishing Agency) issued a complete edition of Dostoievsky's 'artistic works' in 13 volumes (Leningrad, 1926–30), and, more recently, in ten volumes, under the editorship of L. P. Grossman, A. S. Dolinin, V. V. Yermilov and others (Moscow, 1956–8). In the meantime, a number of editions of Dostoievsky's complete works in the original Russian appeared outside the Soviet Union: in the early 1920s in Berlin, in the 1930s in Paris, and in the middle 1940s again in Paris ('YMCA–Press').

In English the 12 volumes of 'The Novels of Fyodor Dostoevsky' translated from the original by Constance Garnett are the nearest approach to a complete edition (W. Heinemann, London 1912–20). They are now supplemented by two volumes of Dostoievsky's *Diary of a Writer*, translated and annotated by Boris Brasol (Cassell, London, 1949), and by a volume of his *Occasional Writings*, selected, translated and introduced by David Magarshack

(Vision Press, London, 1964). Also noteworthy are Magarshack's new translations of Dostoievsky's great books: *Crime and Punishment, The Devils* (i.e. *The Possessed*), *The Idiot,* and *The Brothers Karamazov* (all in the collection 'The Penguin Classics'). The survey *Dostoevsky in English* compiled by Maurice Beebe and Christopher Newton contains a detailed 'checklist' of available translations (in *Modern Fiction Studies,* IV, 1958).

Letters

The standard Russian edition of Dostoievsky's correspondence is: *F. M. Dostoievsky, Pisma,* Vols. I–IV, published and annotated by A. S. Dolinin (Moscow–Leningrad, 1928, 1930, 1934, 1959).

In English the first noteworthy collection of Dostoievsky's letters, translated from the original by S. S. Kotelianski and J. Middleton Murry, appeared in 1923 (Chatto and Windus, London). More comprehensive is the collection *Letters of Fyodor Michailovitch Dostoevsky,* translated by Ethel Colburn Mayne (Peter Owen, London, 1962). Jessie Coulson's volume *Dostoevsky, A Self-Portrait,* with a most useful bibliographical introduction, contains a wealth of extracts from the letters in chronological order (Oxford University Press, London, 1962).

A full edition of the letters in four volumes appeared in French under the title *La Correspondance de Dostoïevski,* translated by Dominique Arban and Nina Gourfinkel (Calman-Lévy, Paris, 1949–61).

(Author's note: To preserve the uniformity of

Dostoievsky's singular philosophical terminology, the author of the present essay translated anew all the quoted passages.)

Biographical and Critical Studies in English

Berdyaev, N. A.: *Dostoievsky, an Interpretation* (transl. from the French, London, 1934).

Berlin, Isaiah: *The Hedgehog and the Fox* (London, 1953).

Carr, E. H.: *Dostoevsky, 1821–1881* (London, 1962).

Dostoevskaya, Anna: *Dostoevsky Portrayed by his Wife* (transl. from the Russian by S. S. Koteliansky, London, 1926).

Dostoevskaya, Lyubov: *Fyodor Dostoyevsky, A Study* (by his daughter, London, 1921).

Freud, Sigmund: *Dostoevsky and Parricide* (London, 1947).

Fueloep-Miller, René: *Fyodor Dostoevsky, Insight, Faith and Prophecy* (transl. from the German, London, 1950).

Gifford, Henry: *The Novel in Russia* (London, 1964).

Hingley, Ronald: *The Undiscovered Dostoyevsky* (London, 1962).

Ivanov, Vyacheslav: *Freedom and the Tragic Life, A Study in Dostoevsky* (transl. from the Russian, London, 1952).

Lavrin, Janko: *Dostoevsky, A Study* (London, 1943).

Magarshack, David: *Dostoevsky, A Life* (London, 1962).

Meier-Graefe, A. J.: *Dostoevsky, the Man and his Work* (transl. from the German, London, 1928).

Merezhkovsky, D. S.: *Tolstoy as Man and Artist, with*

an Essay on Dostoievsky (transl. from the Russian, Westminster, 1902.)

Muchnic, Helen: *Dostoevsky's English Reputation (1881–1936)* in 'Smith College Studies in Modern Languages', vol. XX, (Northampton, Mass., 1939).

Murry, John Middleton: *Fyodor Dostoevsky, a Critical Study* (London, 1924).

Phelps, Gilbert: *The Russian Novel in English Fiction* (London, 1956).

Reeve, F. D.: *The Russian Novel* (London, 1967).

Seduro, Vladimir: *Dostoyevski in Russian Literary Criticism, 1846–1956* (New York, 1957).

Simmons, Ernest J.: *Dostoevsky, the Making of a Novelist* (London, 1950).

Slonim, Marc: *The Three Loves of Dostoyevsky* (New York, 1957).

Steiner, George: *Tolstoy or Dostoievsky* (London, 1960).

Steiner, George: *Tolstoy or Dostoevsky* (London, 1960).

Troyat, Henri: *Firebrand, The Life of Dostoevsky* (transl. from the French, London, 1946).

Wellek, René (editor): *Dostoevsky, a Collection of Critical Essays* (Englewood Cliffs, N. J., 1962).

Yermilov, V.: *Fyodor Dostoyevsky, 1821–1881.* (English translation from the Russian, published in Moscow, 1960.)

Zernov, Nicolas: *Three Russian Prophets* (London, 1944).

Zweig, Stefan: *Master Builders* (transl. from the German, New York, 1930).

In French

Eng, J. van der: *Dostoevskij Romancier* ('s-Gravenhage, 1957).

Gide, André: *Dostoïevsky* (Paris, 1923; English translation with introduction by Arnold Bennett, London, 1925).

Girard, René: *Dostoïevski, Du double à l'unité* (Paris, 1963).

Gourfinkel, Nina: *Dostoïevski notre contemporain* (Paris, 1961).

Guardini, Romano: *L'Univers religieux de Dostoïevski* (transl. from the German, Paris, 1962).

Madaule, Jaques: *Dostoïevski* (Paris, 1956).

Motchoulski, Constantin: *Dostoïevski* (transl. from the Russian, Paris, 1962).

Suarés, André: *Dostoïevski* (Paris, 1911).

Vogüé, E.-M. de: *Le roman russe* (Paris, 1886).

(In addition it may be mentioned that in 1923 the author of the present essay published a book in Russian on Dostoievsky's philosophy entitled *Sistema svobody F. M. Dostoievskovo* (Verlag 'Skythen', Berlin); a German version of this book was published in 1936 by the Vita Nova Verlag in Luzern, Switzerland, under the title *Die Idee der Freiheit – ein Dostojewskij-Buch.*)